Reading the Naked Truth

Literacy, Legislation, and Lies

Gerald Coles

HEINEMANN ■ Portsmouth, NH

Heinemann
A division of Reed Elsevier Inc.
361 Hanover Street
Portsmouth, NH 03801–3912
www.heinemann.com

Offices and agents throughout the world

Library of Congress Cataloging-in-Publication Data
Coles, Gerald.
    Reading the naked truth : literacy, legislation, and lies / Gerald Coles.
      p. cm.
    Includes bibliographical references and index.
    ISBN 0-325-00337-8 (alk. paper)
    1. National Reading Panel (U.S.) Report.   2. Reading—Phonetic method—United States.   3. Reading—Language experience approach—United States.
4. Reading—Research—United States.   5. Reading—Law and legislation—United States.   I. Title.

LB1573.3 .C65 2003
372.46'5—dc21   2002014591

Editor: Lois Bridges
Production: Vicki Kasabian
Cover design: Night and Day Design
Typesetter: Argosy
Manufacturing: Steve Bernier

Printed in the United States of America on acid-free paper
07 06 05 04 03 VP 1 2 3 4 5

To Rom, Terry, Jeremy, and Walter ...

"Beat on the drum and blow the fife"
Heinrich Heine

ontents

Acknowledgments

In their steadfast commitment to sound teaching and learning, and in opposition to the assault on education, countless teachers throughout the United States and in other countries (Australia, New Zealand, Canada, England, Israel—to name but a few) have opposed the legislation mandating authoritarian and harmful prepackaged reading instruction. These teachers have been learning about the so-called scientific research used to justify restrictive mandates, such as those contained in the educational legislation of George W. Bush. They read books and articles on sound teaching. They share information with colleagues. They support one another. They organize conferences that include alternative viewpoints. They speak out individually and in groups against these mandates. But most of all, they continue to insist upon using sound teaching in their classrooms. Sometimes this means going against the grain, feigning to teach the anemic, scripted lessons but actually providing their students rich literacy learning behind the closed classroom door. And sometimes it means yielding to the mandated instruction; adding as much sound teaching as possible within compulsory constraints; enduring until the failures of the mandated pedagogy become evident; hoping and working to make sound teaching prevail.

My thanks to these teachers not only for what they have done for children but for what they have given me. During the last few years I have spent more time than I could have ever imagined reading and writing about the empirical research related to the mandates. Through this often tedious, sometimes exasperating work, I have been in contact with these teachers in conferences, Internet discussions, and so on, and their determination and commitment have helped sustain me. Always I have felt, to paraphrase Robert Frost, "we work together, I tell them from the heart, whether we work together or apart."

Also determined and committed is my editor, Lois Bridges (the editor who never sleeps). Along with offering her keen editorial eye, she has encouraged and supported books that have helped counter the attack on literacy education and promote good teaching. Lois truly is a tree standing by the water that shall not be moved.

Much appreciation to Maura Sullivan, Vicki Kasabian, and Leigh Peake for their many contributions to this second Heinemann book.

For his fellowship in being the only other person in the universe who has actually read end to end the pseudoscience I discuss in this and my previous book, and for his many kinds of help, a special thanks to Steve Krashen.

Thanks also are extended to Elaine Garan, not only for her help but for so often standing up as a majority of one.

Joanne Yatvin has shown principled courage as the sole dissenting voice on the National Reading Panel and as a whistle-blower revealing the Panel's deficient processes in contriving its report. She deserves profuse appreciation, and she certainly has mine.

And always, for Maria Tova, love and poet, whose work, understanding, and compassion are embodied in the twenty-two letters referred to in the Sefer Yezirah (The Book of Creation, the first Kabbalah text), letters filled first and foremost with *meanings*: "Twenty-two letters: Engrave them, carve them, weigh them, permute them, and transform them, and with them depict the soul of all that was formed and all that will be formed in the future."

The Road to Mandating Instruction and Ending "Wiggle Room"

cientifically based reading instruction! A national report has identified the scientific evidence that should be applied to all classrooms! At last the nation has an instructional solution for its
reading problems! These have been typical pronouncements for the
"grand goals" that George W. Bush described when signing federal
reading legislation making this "scientifically based reading instruction" the legislative standard and instrument for ensuring that all
children learn to read.

Right after becoming president in January 2001, Bush sent
Congress an educational reform "blueprint"—Reading First—that
promised to eliminate the nation's "reading deficit" by "ensuring that
every child can read by the third grade." To do so, he proposed
applying "the findings of years of scientific research on reading" to
"all schools in America." Bush stressed that these findings were "now
available," especially in the recently published report of the National
Reading Panel (NRP), which, having reviewed "100,000 studies on
how students learn to read," had provided a guide for the "scientifically based reading instruction" contained in his legislation.[1] Bush
admonished that his legislation would provide funds for reading
instruction—but only if the instruction was scientifically based.
Before scientifically based reading instruction was given its place at

the federal level, this powerful concept had been used effectively to influence reading instruction through state and local policy and legislation in the United States and through national legislation in countries as far away as New Zealand and Israel.

Bush admonished that his legislation would provide funds for reading instruction—but only if the instruction was scientifically based.

In January 2002, Bush began his second year in office by signing educational legislation—the reauthorization of the Elementary and Secondary Education Act, titled No Child Left Behind Act of 2001 (H.R. 1)—saying[2]:

> We're going to spend more money, more resources, but they'll be directed at methods that work, not feel-good methods, not sound-good methods, but methods that actually work, particularly when it comes to reading. So this bill focuses on reading. It sets a grand goal for the children. Our children will be reading by the third grade. And so, therefore, we tripled the amount of federal funding for scientifically based early reading programs. We've got money in there to make sure teachers know how to teach what works. We've got money in there to help promote proven methods of instruction. There are no more excuses, as far as I'm concerned, about not teaching children how to read. We know what works.[3]

"Scientifically based reading instruction" appears nearly fifty times in the legislation. Schools applying for the reading funds will have to explain how they will craft their teaching and curriculum according to this standard. Many applicants will likely carefully omit instruction and educational research they endorse, and educational researchers they respect, because they know what is blacklisted from the realm of "scientific" reading instruction. Mere mention of them might flag an application for quick rejection. Beyond a chilling influence on applicants, the legislation will further shape both conventional educational and public wisdom about what is and is not scientifically based reading instruction.

The instruction that is supposed to work is stepwise, direct, explicit, and systematic skills-emphasis teaching that proceeds from sounds, to letter-sound relationships (i.e., phonics), to word identification, to reading fluency—moving skill-by-skill steadily toward comprehension and eventually (so the model asserts) reaching it. This instruction comes conveniently packaged in commercially produced reading programs that include textbooks and an array of instructional materials. Teachers, serving as middle managers and adhering to the preplanned lesson sequence in a teacher's manual, will not have to worry about anything as they lead their students lesson after lesson, skill after skill.

Accompanying this instruction are claims that have assailed teachers and the public. General statements about the so-called scientific findings of the National Reading Panel Report and the superiority of scientific reading instruction are repeated in the media and in policy discussions without a modicum of doubt, and alternative views seldom appear in public discussions to counter these assumptions—assumptions repeated to the point of becoming truisms. Astonishingly, given the impact the reading legislation can have on children's literacy outcomes, these truisms are voiced with little, if any, examination of the body of research that is supposed to be their foundation, and often with the utmost disdain for anything outside of them.

While writing this book, I have given several talks to teachers and have always begun with two questions: "If you feel you have an adequate understanding of the Bush reading legislation, would you raise a hand?" and "If you feel you have an adequate understanding of the National Reading Panel Report cited in the legislation, would you raise a hand?" Seldom was a hand raised in response to these questions. Such responses were not surprising, given the meager information on the legislation and the NRP Report that has appeared in the media. Readers of a few professional journals such as *Kappan*, *Education Week*, and *Rethinking Schools* might have read articles and letters on these issues, but unless teachers had subscribed to and read these journals, they might easily have missed such discussions.

What they were likely to see is illustrated in a column by Brent Staples in the *New York Times* published the day before Bush signed the educational legislation.[4] The "good news" for children who might have reading problems, Staples stated, is that findings from the National Institute of Child Health and Human Development (NICHD) show "that 95 percent of learning-impaired children can become effective readers if taught by scientifically proven methods." At the same time, whole language—an approach in which teachers help students learn to read by integrating all facets of written language, rather than moving stepwise from one skill to another—is caricatured in the article as a "fad of the 1970s, in which children were allowed to wander through books, improvising individual approaches to reading." Unmentioned in Staples' assertions are (a) the failure of the NICHD to demonstrate any scientifically proven methods, (b) the nonexistence of a single NICHD-supported study—regardless of its validity—that claimed a 95 percent success rate, (c) the failure of NICHD to demonstrate that its scientific methods of instruction have yielded superior reading success for either normal readers or those said to be learning impaired, and (d) the existence of ample writings and research that would reveal that his depiction of whole language is caricature or at least disputable.[5]

In state and federal hearings, usually controlled by champions of this so-called scientific instruction, all but like-minded advocates are excluded. One need only look, for example, at the list of speakers who have appeared at hearings of the House Committee on Education and the Workforce, the same committee that wrote the federal reading legislation and whose members and staff helped move this legislation through Congress. Only those who have showered praise on scientific reading instruction have entered the hearing room doors (e.g., Reid Lyon, Joseph Torgesen, and Louisa Moats of NICHD; Linda Schrenko, Georgia state superintendent of schools; Donald N. Langenberg, chair of the NRP; Diane Ravitch, a member of several conservative policy institutes; and assorted teachers testifying to the effectiveness of phonics and similar skills in their classrooms).[6]

> Only those advocates of skills-emphasis teaching who have showered praise on scientific reading instruction have entered the hearing room doors.

Business councils seeking to influence reading education across the country have promoted only the "scientific" view. In 1996, for example, the Texas business council, after deciding it "wanted to find out what worked before they did anything," assembled and paid a group of "experts" at a Houston Reading Summit so that the business council could "find out who the good speakers were, to know who [sic] to invite back, and to begin to get familiar with the research in reading." Only experts in the scientific view (Reid Lyon, Bonnie Grossen, Doug Carnine, Jack Fletcher, Jean Osborne, Barbara Foorman) were invited to join the payroll, suggesting that before the summit was organized, the council had already decided what worked. After the experts established that "there is clear research that direct instruction in phonemic and phonological awareness makes a difference in getting kids to read," the business council "then did a statewide reading conference to expand on the horizon" and afterward "launched the initiative statewide."[7]

The Best Available Science

Shortly after George W. Bush sent Congress his reading proposal that called for legislation that would apply "the findings of years of scientific research on reading" to "all schools in America," he rejected a policy for reducing carbon dioxide emissions in power plants because, he said, the science was "still incomplete."[8] He also terminated plans to reduce the amount of arsenic in drinking water so that, he said, his administration could "make a decision based on sound science."[9] He went on to withdraw the United States from the international agreement to reduce global warming because, he insisted, the "state of scientific knowledge of the causes of, and solutions to global climate change" was "incomplete."[10]

Never has this nation had a more scientifically minded president. These decisions suggest that Bush has studied an array of scientific literature and has been able to formulate policy judgments based on the empirical evidence. One might conclude, therefore, that the reading research must indeed be sound for the president to have given it his one empirical imprimatur.

On the other hand, his imprimatur seems to have been based largely on intuition. Just before signing the final legislation in Ohio, Bush said, "It's not exactly light reading." He then signed it, flew to Boston, and said in a speech there, "I wish you could have seen the piece of legislation. It's really tall. And I admit, I haven't read it yet. You'll be happy to hear I don't intend to." But, he assured his audience, he didn't have to, because he knew "the principles behind the bill," one of which was to spend "money for early reading programs based upon the science of reading, not something that sounds good or feels good, but something that works."[11]

> Bush said, "I haven't read [this reading education legislation] yet. You'll be happy to hear I don't intend to."

Perhaps he felt confident that he knew the principles because the Texas "educational miracle" over which he presided had, after all, already implemented scientific reading instruction. Bush had selected Rod Paige to be secretary of education, for example, because of his reported success as superintendent of the Houston, Texas, schools in "turning around the nation's seventh-largest school district," as evidenced in the district's "dramatic increase in test scores," an achievement partly attributable, said ABC News, to Houston's shift "toward phonics-based reading instruction."[12] During his nomination hearing, Paige observed that "too many schools are not teaching children basic skills such as reading and writing."[13] "I believe that reading is the gateway to learning," he said, and vowed "I'll work to ensure that every disadvantaged child—and every child—can learn to read."[14]

When Paige addressed the national meeting of the International Reading Association a few months after becoming secretary of education, he robustly reiterated the scientific view, indicating that he too was familiar with the principles in the Bush reading legislation. The administration's commitment "to ensuring that every child can read by the third grade," he told his audience, would be met by reading legislation that would provide funds to states and local school districts "to implement comprehensive, research-based, proven methods of teaching reading." Paige's talk, filled with references to science, research, and research-based and science-based reading instruction, cited the National Reading Panel Report as the document establishing these "proven methods": having "screened more than 100,000 studies of reading" and using "a rigorous research standard," the Panel had "found the most effective course of reading instruction."[15]

A Closer Look at Scientific Reading Instruction

Education Week reporter Kathleen Manzo described basic reading education in Houston as "drilling in Texas": teachers "are marching in lockstep to fulfill district orders that basic skills make up the core of their reading instruction." Classes immerse the city's poorest children in a "highly scripted program" using exercises "designed to teach youngsters to read through an intense focus on explicit, systematic phonics." The "structured reading tasks" link "repetitive phonics activities" with "stories that correspond to each lesson." As Manzo describes it, the Houston schools "have taken an almost militaristic stand" on reading instruction that "has forced teachers in every one of the district's 280 elementary, middle, and high schools to conform to a more uniform strategy for teaching reading that begins with basic skills."[16]

This direct, explicit, and systematic instruction of skills has sometimes been called "phonics teaching," a phrase that captures the instruction's word-skills emphasis but is not a precise description because, although phonics is a major component of the skills taught, it is only one of them. Furthermore, how this instruction is administered is as important as the content that is delivered. As the description of Houston instruction reveals, scientific instruction is predicated on the assumption that learning to read requires mastery of a sequence of skills, each building upon the other, and all taught directly, explicitly, and systematically. The preplanned, published reading programs are designed to demand and ensure proper content and sequence and thereby help "teacher-proof" instruction. The programs further promote teacher-proofing by providing a test gauge that administrators can use to appraise teachers' adherence to the scientifically based script.

> *The preplanned reading programs are designed to "teacher-proof" instruction.*

The initial skill in the sequence, according to the NRP Report, is phonemic awareness—the ability to manipulate phonemes, the smallest units of speech sounds, as when blending or separating phonemes in order to identify words. Teaching children phonemic awareness, the NRP Report advises, "was highly effective under a variety of teaching conditions with a variety of learners across a range of grade and age levels" because it "significantly improves their reading more than instruction that lacks any attention" to phonemic awareness. Systematic phonics instruction is next in the sequence because, the Report maintains, it "produces significant benefits for students in kindergarten through 6th grade and for children having difficulty learning to read."[17] Examination of the research on phonics, the NRP Report concludes, supports reading educator Jeanne Chall's "assertion that early instruction in systematic phonics is especially beneficial to growth in reading."[18] Next in the instructional sequence is fluency—reading orally with speed, accuracy, and proper expression. And so on, from skill to skill, from small parts of language to large ones, minimizing reading for meaning and comprehension until all prerequisite skills are learned. The sequence of skills never runs in the opposite direction, that is, from comprehension to skills, and the ingredients that constitute beginning reading are never described as interactive from the very start of learning to read, although, as I will discuss in the next chapter, the latter model is a valid one in reading education.

Scientific instruction moves from skill to skill, minimizing comprehension.

While advocates of this stepwise instruction insist it is balanced, that is, the instruction balances learning skills for reading with reading for meaning, a close look reveals that the meaning and comprehension end of this "balance" remains very much out-of-balance.

Indicative of the balance in this scientific instruction is the NICHD press release announcing the NRP Report. In the title and body of the press release, the term *comprehension* was referred to seven times and *thinking* zero times, compared with the twenty-nine times that skills terms (*phonics, phonemic awareness, phonemes,* and *sounds*) were used to describe the Report's findings. For units of language emphasized in the press release, *word* or *words* was mentioned nine times, compared with the complete absence of any larger language units, such as *sentence, paragraph, story,* or *book.* Overall, the press release reflected the reigning scientific instructional method that is vivid in the reading legislation.[19] The "components" of reading are enumerated in a list that starts with phonemic awareness, is followed by phonics, continues through vocabulary and reading fluency, and ends with reading comprehension.

The Context of the "Most Effective Way"

An adequate appraisal of the instruction advocated in the NRP Report is impossible without first placing the document itself in both historical and present context. Rather than accepting the reasoning provided by its proponents, understanding the report requires knowing what prompted the formation and composition of the NRP and what social and educational forces and purposes the report serves. As I discussed in *Reading Lessons: The Debate Over Literacy* (1998), conflicts over how to teach reading have continued in various forms for more than two centuries: arguments have ensued over whether reading instruction should emphasize meaning or skills; how reading instruction affects and should be affected by students' interests, motivation, and enthusiasm; whether reading, writing, and spelling should be regarded as independent or connected subjects;

and so forth. Embedded in all these conflicts were practical and theoretical differences over how children learn best and what the aims of education and children's development should be.[20]

With the rise of reading research around 1910, arguments over instruction began to include references to scientific, pragmatic studies on what worked best in instruction and references to more basic research attempting to determine which kinds of reading instruction would be most congruent with children's mental operations.

Although the influence of this research varied among school systems, schools, and classroom teachers, it was never *the* determining factor for making curriculum choices. Most often, curriculum was determined by a combination of considerations, especially by the prominence and reputations of published reading programs and the practical judgments educators made about the effectiveness of reading programs used in their schools and classrooms. These programs were developed with the consultation of reading experts who had their own ideas about the research findings that ought to be used in creating reading textbooks and materials (test questions, worksheets, etc.). Nevertheless, different sides in the debate over reading agreed—for different reasons—that the creation of these programs was governed by much more than scientific evidence.

Jeanne Chall, for example, a reading educator whose career was dedicated to making code emphasis (i.e., phonics) the core of beginning reading instruction, analyzed reading textbook series in the late 1960s and complained that they gave "only minor attention to the alphabetic-phonics aspects" of words, despite "the experimental, correlational, and clinical evidence" indicating "that a code emphasis is a better way to start" learning to read.[21] Similarly, but with a different view of the evidence, educators with a whole language orientation concluded that at best, the "process of producing" these programs is a

> highly conservative one. It inhibits any real change or innovation as it seeks to minimize risks in sales and profits. This makes it hard for authors, editors, or even management to incorporate newly discovered knowledge from theory and research, since the potential response of [reading program] selection committees cannot be predicted safely.[22]

These two approaches to reading instruction, while expressing a similar dissatisfaction with the exclusion of research in formulating instructional materials, contain an important difference in appraising the contribution each side believed research can make. While Chall made her case for a heavy emphasis on code instruction solely on what she claimed were several kinds of research evidence, the whole language statement invoked *both* research and theory: scientific studies were important for creating and selecting instruction, but so too was reasoning formulated from facts and interpretations contained in a variety of sources.

The antecedents to the NRP Report and the politics connected to it can be traced through national reports on reading over the last three decades, reading legislation and policy at various governmental levels, media stories on reading, and reading research.[23] I have put reading research at the end of the list to indicate its relative importance among these antecedents; that is, it has been the *use* of certain kinds of reading research, not the existence of compelling findings of certain reading research, that has helped create the final answer to beginning reading instruction.

> *There are no compelling findings in reading research that have helped create the final answer to beginning reading instruction.*

For more than a decade prior to the Bush legislation, skills-instruction boosters have sought to incorporate phonics and related skills language into federal legislation. Following the circulation of a Republican policy paper in 1989, a new provision in the 1990 Adult Literacy Act included phonics in a list of instructional methods eligible for federal funds, and the chair of the Republican Policy Committee hailed the provision as a great victory, stating, "Research shows phonics is the most effective way to teach people to read."[24] Nevertheless, resistance to this effort appeared in a 1994 Congressional educational bill that contained the statement, "The disproven theory that children must first learn basic skills before engaging in more complex tasks continues to dominate strategies for classroom instruction, resulting in emphasis on repetitive drill and practice at the expense of content-rich instruction, accelerated curricula, and effective teaching to high standards." Incensed by this counterattack, skills advocates rallied through a mail campaign that made congressional supporters of the bill worry that they might appear to be anti-phonics and, therefore, anti-education, and the statement was subsequently dropped from the final legislative version.[25]

Scientific beginning reading instruction took a major leap forward in 1998 when Congress passed the Reading Excellence Act, legislation that required funding only for reading instruction based on reliable research. At the forefront of the definition of beginning reading achievement were "the skills and knowledge to understand how phonemes, or speech sounds, are connected to print" and "the ability to decode unfamiliar words."[26]

The national reports accompanying these developments span from Secretary of Education William J. Bennett's 1986 report, *First Lessons*,[27] recommending the use of available "knowledge about the basic processes of reading," which included explicit phonics instruction, to *Preventing Reading Difficulties in Young Children*, a National Academy of Science report published in 1998 that seemed to call for balance but urged heavy skills teaching in beginning reading.[28] Echoing the "findings" of these reports were articles in media, such as the *Los Angeles Times*, *Atlantic*, the *Baltimore Sun*, the *Washington Post*, and the Heritage Foundation's *Policy Review*, all attacking whole language and other "feel-good" teaching practices and calling for no-nonsense scientifically based reading instruction.

These efforts to establish uniform reading instruction need to be seen within the attack on the type of education that emerged in the 1960s—an attack that has sought, with considerable success, to eliminate the cultural changes that during these years began to redefine schooling. These changes included more power for teachers and students, such as giving students greater voice in formulating the direction of instruction, reducing school and classroom hierarchy and increasing democratic decision making, encouraging students' critical thinking, and giving greater classroom attention to issues of equality and justice. As educator Ira Shor documents, this attack drummed up a "literacy crisis and back-to-basics" campaign that began in 1975,[29] with the concepts of this effort—concepts such as excellence, standards, accountability, and research—taking on an apolitical character that cloaked the attack's formidable conservative political makeup.

> The present attack on reading reforms can be traced back to a drummed-up "back-to-basics" campaign that began in 1975.

Within the efforts to redefine schooling during these years, the whole language movement developed as a grassroots effort that emphasized teacher decision making in the classroom and learning that was "more collaborative, inquiry-based, meaning-centered" and that valued "student experience and knowledge." It was a movement that critiqued conventional schooling and its "testing, tracking, standardization, and imposed curriculum" and that embraced a concern for "educational and social justice." The movement's educational, social, and theoretical concerns were soon weakened, however, as attacks against it grew and as educators with minimal understanding of the movement's fundamentals identified themselves as whole language. The attacks increased pressure enough so that classroom teaching that strayed from orthodoxy became increasingly difficult to practice and what became identified as whole language in many classrooms was no more than limited to mild changes in "methods and materials."[30] For all the dilution, however, the qualities embedded in whole language—and their potential "menace"—were not lost on those upholding the status quo. As educators Paula Wolfe and Leslie Poyner emphasize, all teaching and learning operate within a large structure organized around "specific sociocultural, political, and economic intentions." Hence, any educational innovations, such as whole language, that challenge or appear to challenge this dominant structure become a "political threat to the status quo" and are countered by efforts to marginalize, discount, or appropriate instructional innovations and thereby "lessen their political threat to the status quo."[31]

The NICHD Role in Promoting the "Good News"

The apolitical-research-as-final-arbiter stratagem within which the "scientifically based reading instruction" mandates are cloaked has been fortified by the Child Development and Behavior branch of the NICHD at the National Institutes of Health (NIH). That branch, responsible for reading research and headed by G. Reid Lyon, has in recent years been regarded by skills-education advocates as the research organization that has funded "gold standard" scientific studies on beginning reading. It has funded a plethora of studies in forty-one university research sites across the country (e.g., Florida State University, Georgetown University, University of Texas, University of Colorado, University of Washington-Seattle); these sites, according to Lyon, "have been deployed to identify what it takes to learn to read, to delineate the factors that impede robust reading development, and to determine how best to prevent and remediate reading failure."[32]

Although Lyon is described as a research psychologist, specialist in reading development, and in other apolitical professional terms, these descriptions fail to convey his decidedly political qualities that have helped transform the NICHD "science" on reading into law. As the *Wall Street Journal* reported, he and George W. Bush

> have had a long and fruitful, if little-noticed, relationship. In Texas, Mr. Lyon helped design and sell a Bush plan to revamp how public-school students are taught to read. As president, Mr. Bush is turning to his phonics mentor to expand the program nationally. Mr. Lyon is "the reading guru," Mr. Bush told a meeting of business leaders in January. Reading czar may be more accurate.

Lyon has been an adviser to Bush since 1995, when Mr. Bush's aides discovered that a researcher funded by Lyon's division was "studying Houston school children and concluding that phonics instruction was effective." After discussing the NICHD findings with the Texas governor, Lyon "traveled to Texas at least 10 times during the next four years to promote the Bush" educational plan.[33] After Bush became president, Lyon worked "with Republican congressional aides to craft Mr. Bush's reading initiative" and "wrote most of the reading portions" of the bill.[34]

My last book, *Misreading Reading: The Bad Science That Hurts Children*, reviewed the research either funded by the NICHD or cited by NICHD spokespersons and researchers as evidence for the heavy skills teaching they advocate and concluded that this body of studies does not support claims made about it.[35] These studies were rife with deficiencies in design and reasoning and had a strong tendency to make a case for skills teaching regardless of the data, and a number of the studies actually provided support for conclusions contrary to the claims NICHD spokespersons made about them.

> *The studies cited by NICHD spokespersons that supposedly support skills teaching are rife with deficiencies in design and reasoning.*

Despite the lack of scientific substantiation, the NICHD assertions have helped achieve political aims. In California, for example, state school board member Marion Joseph recalls "urging people to study the research on beginning reading," especially the "NICHD reports on reading," which "stated unequivocally that beginning readers needed phonemic awareness [the ability to hear and manipulate sounds in words] as a prerequisite for learning to decode. It also told us that good readers are fluent and automatic decoders and poor readers overly rely on context." Despite initial resistance to her efforts to change what was "very wrong" in reading instruction, Joseph "didn't despair" about improving reading education in California, because she "knew that there was [sic] massive amounts of research that brought us good news." Armed with this "good news," Joseph helped establish a state mandate requiring the "systematic, explicit instruction in the alphabetic code" in beginning reading instruction. "I felt so strongly in the efficacy of the alphabetic principle," she effused, "that I called it 'the best invention of civilization.'"[36]

> California mandates the "systematic, explicit instruction" in "the best invention of civilization," the alphabetic code.

Like everyone else promoting scientific reading instruction, Lyon claims that the NICHD research promotes a balanced approach to reading instruction. But, educational researchers Richard Allington and Michael Pressley observed,

> As we reviewed the list of 2,500 NICHD-supported articles, we detected much less attention to these higher-order processes related to comprehension than to more atomistic components of reading, such as sound-, letter-, and word-skills. Moreover, when we have been in the company of NICHD-supported researchers and leadership, there has been much too little discussion above the word level. It is easy to leave NICHD-driven discussions with the impression that sound-, letter-, and word-level processes are all that really matters in reading, that if sound-, letter-, and word-level processes could be solved, literacy problems would be solved.[37]

In an interview, Lyon was asked to "explain the steps involved in learning to read." "A major prerequisite for learning to read an alphabetic language like English is to understand that the words we use in our speech are actually composed of individual sounds," Lyon responded.

"So the sounds are like atoms, and the words are molecules?" the interviewer queried.

"Exactly," Lyon answered. *"The individual sounds are called phonemes, which beginning readers learn before proceeding to text"* (my emphasis).

> But those squiggly lines on the page really don't mean anything until the brain hooks them to sounds and then links those sounds together to form words. As youngsters are learning to read, they'll use this phoneme awareness to develop what's called the alphabetic principle, which is an understanding that the print in front of you is, in fact, linked to various sounds. As a child's coming along, he's never seen the word *bag* before, and what he has to learn is that the *b* written symbol goes with the sound /b/ and the *a* goes with the sound /a/ and so forth, and that's how a child learns to decode the sound.

Condensing Lyon's explanation, the interviewer replied, "The linking of sounds to letters is the phonics part?"

"Right," Lyon affirmed. Asked to explain why reading is not "being taught well in so many of our schools," Lyon repeated the NICHD mantra, "A great deal of it is related to the tendency in education to develop teaching practices based on philosophy rather than on science."[38]

Lyon's claim about the science upholding the NICHD brand of reading instruction versus the philosophy propping all opposition has been echoed by those whose work is funded by the NICHD. In *Teaching Reading IS Rocket Science: What Expert Teachers of Reading Should Know and Be Able to Do*, NICHD-supported researcher Louisa Moats opened her position paper with the assertion, "Thanks to new scientific research—plus a long-awaited scientific and political consensus around this research—the knowledge exists to teach all but a handful of severely disabled children to read well." She continued, "We now know that classroom teaching itself, when it includes a range of research-based components and practices, can prevent and ameliorate reading difficulty"; "research should guide the profession."[39] Most of the research Moats cited was NICHD-funded; the rest reinforced the NICHD conclusions. No alternative views were in the paper; presumably, any researcher disinclined to join the "consensus" was not worth mentioning. One revealing part of Moats'—and, by implication, the NICHD's—perspective is her phrase "political consensus." As I have said, supposedly the apolitical scientific consensus has won the day. The phrase "political consensus" discloses, however, what is apparent to everyone observing the narrowly scoped political efforts forging scientific reading instruction: the enforcement of instruction that has been instituted by not giving educators and parents full information and an opportunity to choose.

A purported scientific-political consensus enforces instruction that gives educators and parents no choice.

Continuing the course of this trajectory has not been altogether easy for the NICHD reading researchers and the forces they represent. Because the legitimacy of the political consensus rests on a perceived "validity of scientific reading instruction," the NICHD—leading the establishment of this perceived validity—has been in the awkward position of appearing self-serving in anointing its own research as the premier evidence. Needed has been a third party to sanction the NICHD enterprise—a panel of experts, for example, who would stand above the fray of the reading wars and settle the matter once and for all by putting a stamp of approval on the NICHD viewpoint.

Ending "Wiggle Room"

The first such panel, even though created through the National Academy of Science, was extensively shaped by the NICHD: the NICHD partly funded it, and half its members were NICHD-supported researchers or others closely aligned with them. Considering this NICHD influence, both advocates and critics of the NICHD research anticipated that the report, *Preventing Reading Difficulties in Young Children*, would provide a clear endorsement of the NICHD viewpoint.[40] Whether or not it did is open to question, but, unexpectedly, the contrary views of a few committee members forced a modicum of compromise in the final report, enabling educators to interpret portions of the report as recommending a balanced approach that could include stepwise skills-emphasis reading instruction—but need not. Moreover, many educators interpreted the report as one that underscored the responsibility of teachers to determine what skills their students needed and how these skills should be taught, an interpretation perhaps most devastating for the NICHD viewpoint.

The National Council of Teachers of English (NCTE), for example, concluded that the report recognized "that the identical mix of instructional materials and strategies will not work for every child" and that effective teaching requires crafting "a special mix of instructional ingredients for every child." NCTE also felt that rather than advocating a stepwise skills-to-meaning approach in beginning reading, the report maintained "that initial and developmental reading instruction must address meaning as well as knowledge of the alphabetic principle and that children must have frequent opportunities to read in order to achieve fluency."[41]

Lyon's dissatisfaction was obvious in his immediate response to the report. He observed that the report had "gone the farthest of any consensus document" but complained that as a consensus document, it was "ambiguous" and bemoaned that "teachers from different belief systems will probably have the tendency to evaluate this based on their own perspectives." Consensus, for Lyon, did not mean agreeing that different instructional positions have supportive evidence but none has sufficient evidence to nullify all other views.

Lyon's unhappiness was echoed by Louisa Moats, who thought the report "didn't go far enough in stressing the importance of phonemic awareness and explicit phonics in early stages of reading." Like Lyon, she desired a report that precisely recommended the instructional line teachers need to toe: the report "leaves a lot of wiggle room" she complained.[42] As I have said, it is debatable whether in totality the report could be read this way (I thought it gave too much support to the NICHD position). However, for advocates of the NICHD viewpoint, the agency's funding of, involvement in, and representation on the committee had not paid off.

> The prior consensus report, Preventing Reading Difficulties, didn't go far enough in stressing the importance of skills in early reading and in avoiding instructional "wiggle room."

By coincidence—or, as Bob Dylan has written, "take what you can gather from coincidence"—no sooner had *Preventing Reading Difficulties* appeared in 1998 than a new panel was announced, one that would be "chosen by the chiefs of the NICHD and the Department of Education." This panel, Lyon explained, would "identify the types of research methods and evidence that are most useful for informing instructional and policy decisions." It would "suggest the kind of scientific evidence that ought to guide policy and instructional decisions" and would go beyond what Lyon saw as a grave problem: "In the reading community for years there has been the feeling that anybody's research is as good as another's."[43] This panel would eschew consensus.

A week later (March 27, 1998), the NICHD formally announced it had obtained a congressional "request," firstly, to organize a study of "the effectiveness of various approaches to teaching children how to read" and, secondly, to report the "best ways to apply these findings in classrooms and at home."[44] Given the NICHD's considerable congressional connections—especially with conservative Republicans on the House Committee on Education and the Workforce, which had used the NICHD research to justify earlier legislative mandates on reading instruction—saying that the NICHD had received a request is like saying Lockheed Martin Corporation receives a request from the Pentagon to build bombers. That is, that the company CEO and board, without ever lobbying, making campaign contributions, or sitting in chairs that revolve between the company and the Pentagon, unexpectedly receive the request in the mail one fine day.

Soon after the first reading report was published, a new panel was announced, one expected to overcome the problem of "wiggle room."

Duane Alexander, the director of NICHD, later said the following about this request: "NICHD determined the seven questions in its charge through conversations with the original legislation's authors in Congress."[45] The Department of Education was formally included as a consulting organization in this undertaking, but the NICHD spearheaded the selection, organization, and administrative processes of the National Reading Panel, as it was called. All information releases about the Panel flowed from the NICHD, with Duane Alexander the chief spokesperson presenting them. When the panel members were announced, Alexander was the only person on the "selection committee" who was quoted in the press release.

Two years later the Panel finished its work and Alexander announced that "for the first time, we now have guidance—based on evidence from sound scientific research—on how best to teach children to read. The panel's rigorous scientific review identifies the most effective strategies for teaching reading."[46]

Reid Lyon, testifying before the House Committee on Education and the Workforce, reported that the National Reading Panel, using "a set of rigorous research methodology standards by which to judge" the studies it reviewed, "was able to identify instructional approaches that are ready for classroom implementation." Like all of Lyon's appearances before this committee, no one with contrary views was invited to testify along with him.[47]

"How Sweet the Sound"

Among the media announcements of the Panel's report was an article in *USA Today* titled "Friends of Phonics Dance for Joy" and accompanied by a photograph of Sister Marcella Kucia, an eighty-five-year-old nun, dancing with kindergartners while teaching Plaid Phonics. Quoted in the article was a representative of the company that published the program, who observed that the recently released report of the National Reading Panel and its endorsement of phonics "does confirm us." Summing up the joy was the article's subtitle: "How Sweet the Sound of Endorsement, Five Decades Later."[48]

Since the NRP Report had so much to say about phonics, it should be observed that Plaid Phonics, "inspired by the pattern on uniforms worn for decades in Catholic schools throughout the USA," is phonetically irregular. Usually, as everyone who remembers the phonics golden rule knows, when two vowels go walking, the first one does the talking. Therefore, the sound of the vowel combination in *plaid* should be long, as in *laid, main,* or *raisin.* When I first read the phonics program's title using the phonics rule, I thought the name was Played Phonics, not an unreasonable, rule-grounded guess, I think. The inconsistency seemed to suggest something about phonics rules, but neither the publishers of the program nor the author of the newspaper article seemed to notice.

The joyful *USA Today* article was only one of many media reports announcing the Panel's findings and emphasizing, as *Education Week* reported: "Reading Panel Urges Phonics for All in K–6."[49] The report did urge more than phonics in reading instruction, but the headline was generally correct because the Panel stressed that beginning readers should attain an early mastery of sound-symbol connections and similar skills through explicit, systematic, direct instruction.

The *Baltimore Sun* explained that the "National Reading Panel, ordered by Congress two years ago to cull from thousands of studies the most effective teaching methods," sifted "through more than 100,000 studies of reading." Duane Alexander chose Donald Langenberg, the chancellor of the University of Maryland and a physicist, "to head the panel because he had no direct interest in the ideologically charged reading controversies." Similarly, the panel members who were chosen "had not taken strong stands in the reading wars." Describing the findings, Langenberg stressed that "the panel was asked to deal in science, not ideology, and we did our level best to do that." Whether or not this is true I shall discuss in the chapters ahead.[50]

Referring to this report, *USA Today* reprimanded the "nation's teacher colleges" for "ignoring compelling new research" when training teachers. Langenberg explained how "shocked" he was by "the disregard education professors hold for scientific research." As chancellor, he planned "to require that the teacher colleges" at his university "teach reading based on top scientific findings" and would take it upon himself to spread the "message to college presidents, business leaders and teacher unions."[51]

> The head of the NRP vowed to make sure his university would "teach reading based on top scientific findings" from now on.

American Federation of Teachers (AFT) President Sandra Feldman praised the report as "a significant milestone—the first time that this kind of analysis of research on effective reading instruction has been done. It helps solidify our knowledge about what works best in teaching children to read."[52] The International Reading Association commended the Panel's "work in reviewing scientific evidence" and "for pulling together a huge body of work."[53] The *Los Angeles Times* reported that the conclusions of the Panel "reflect a growing consensus among educators that children must be taught how to manipulate the sounds and letters in words, while having ample opportunity to practice these skills by reading books."[54]

A final example of media coverage of the Panel's findings is an editorial in the *Indianapolis Star*, which informed readers that after evaluating "data available from 100,000 research studies conducted since 1966," the Panel had concluded that "the most effective method of teaching children to read is systematic phonics instruction, which means teaching children the sounds of our alphabetic language in an explicit and sequential way. A prerequisite to phonics instruction is awareness of phonemes, the tiniest sounds in our language." The editorial then quoted directly from the NRP Report:

> Systematic phonics instruction produces significant benefits for students in kindergarten through 6th grade and for children having difficulty learning to read. First graders who were taught phonics systematically were better able to decode (sound out words) and spell, and they showed significant improvement in their ability to comprehend text. The effects of systematic early phonics instruction were significant and substantial in kindergarten and the first grade, indicating that systematic phonics programs should be implemented at those age and grade levels.[55]

The Guide to "the Most Important Threads"

The NRP Report had done what it was supposed to have done, while political, professional, and media forces had done the rest. It all was readily transported into the Reading First legislation. The Senate version of the legislation stated:

> Research carried out over the past 2 decades has given us a clear picture of how children learn how to read, what is the cause of reading difficulties, and how instruction can be designed in order to help nearly all children become proficient readers. A recent report of the National Reading Panel, "Teaching Children to Read," summarizes some of the most important threads of this research and presents its implications for instruction. It is this research base that forms the basis on which Reading First is built. All activities carried out with Reading First funds must be based on scientific reading research. The overall focus of Reading First is to have the knowledge generated by solid research reflected in the teaching of reading to all students.[56]

The NRP Report had done what it was supposed to have done.

The recommendations of the NRP report fill the reading section of the final version of the educational legislation (No Child Left Behind, H.R. 1), within which the Reading First legislation is contained, and although the Report is not named in the legislation, the

Conference Report that accompanies it stresses the need to "dramatically increase student achievement" by employing "intensive, research-based learning systems" that "implement the recommendations of the National Reading Panel."[57]

Having laid out the background and context of the reading legislation and the National Reading Panel Report, I will now turn to some specific questions. What were these "100,000 studies"? Who were the members of the National Reading Panel? Did the Panel ask the right questions? Were the views represented on the Panel sufficiently inclusive? Did the NRP satisfactorily answer the congressional mandate?

2   "Diversity" of Views

The Diversity of the Panel

From the nearly three hundred persons nominated by various individuals or organizations, with the stated goal of obtaining "as broad a representation of nominees as possible," the NICHD announced in March 1998 that the fifteen members of the National Reading Panel had been selected and included "prominent reading researchers, teachers, child development experts, leaders in elementary and higher education, and parents."[1] Duane Alexander, head of the NICHD, praised the Panel for its "diversity," its "excellent representation" of "backgrounds" and "areas of focus."[2] The following biographical sketches of the panel members offer an appraisal of the accuracy of Alexander's claim.

> *One NRP panelist was a major NICHD-supported researcher.*

One member was a major NICHD researcher, a recipient of considerable NICHD funding, and a leading member of an NICHD-supported university research site. Anyone familiar with her work would have known there would be no question what "review of the research" she would encourage and what conclusions she would reach. Her participation could have been acceptable, of course, had the Panel included a genuinely broad representation of views—if, for example, there had also been a researcher whose perspective differed from the NICHD model of what counts in beginning reading.

Another panelist, through her active role in various literacy groups at the state and local levels in Texas, had already promoted the NICHD brand of scientific beginning reading instruction and had, in fact, invited researchers supported by NICHD to speak to parents and teachers. This panelist was also on then-Governor George W. Bush's Reading Initiative Taskforce. Should this kind of activist have been on such a panel? The answer could have been yes had the Panel included an activist from a group supporting alternatives to scientific instruction.

Another panelist was on then-Governor Bush's Reading Initiative Taskforce.

A third panelist was an editor of a journal that had devoted an entire issue to NICHD reading research. Guest editors of the special issue were two NICHD-supported reading researchers. With respect to diversity, we can again ask, "Did the Panel include an editor of an educational journal with an alternative viewpoint?"

A fourth panelist's work on the importance of word reading and sound-symbol connections in beginning reading were consonant with that in the NICHD research. The work of another panelist used very narrow models of information processing (e.g., how orthographic information, such as phonemic, visual, and letter-order information, affects comprehension) and included research on reading disabilities that identified phonological awareness problems as key in these disabilities. Similarly, both the sixth and the seventh panelist had done considerable work on a model of the reading process that corresponded with the NICHD paradigm.

Although the writings of another panelist suggested he might serve as a broker for contending sides, a close look at his publications indicated that he was likely to consider the heavy instruction of skills in beginning reading to be a scientifically valid teaching approach and would accept a report that did not include a full appraisal of alternative teaching approaches.

Another panelist had publications sympathetic to views contrary to those in the NICHD research and might have been expected to be the least partisan among the reading researchers. Nonetheless, given the instructional inclination of the Panel, the extent to which this member would actively dissent from the majority opinion was not clear when the Panel was selected.

In addition to the instructional direction in which the reading researchers leaned, most or all of their research was quantitative and empirical, focusing on a small number of variables that influence learning outcomes—the kind of research that the NICHD advocated and funded. There was no member representing other research approaches in reading development, such as qualitative research, ethnographic research, critical literacy research, research on influences outside the classroom that shape teaching and learning in the classroom, whole language research, sociohistorical research, or social process research.

Two additional panelists were educational researchers, but not in reading. One had worked in early childhood development and had studied social competency and self-concept development in kindergarten programs. Another had worked on gender, racial, and ethnic influences and relationships in the classroom. These two members could have been expected to be impartial, but their impartiality depended on being provided a full representation of views in a field outside their areas of expertise.

The same potential impartiality could have been expected of the chair of the Panel, the chancellor of the University of Maryland, and a physicist by profession. Although this member was described as having the "ability to forge consensus on difficult issues," how could he have accomplished this if the Panel's reading researchers did not provide all sides of the difficult issues?

The thirteenth panelist was a middle school teacher in the Houston, Texas, schools, where prominent NICHD research had been done and where, under the leadership of the school system's superintendent, Rod Paige, reading programs consonant with NICHD's instructional views reigned. There was no biographical information disclosing her views on reading education and I could not find any publications she had authored.

Only one panelist, a principal and former teacher, had a clear affiliation with a divergent kind of reading instruction. This panelist had written articles on literacy instruction generally sympathetic to a whole language orientation and a guide for developing a whole language program in schools. By her own admission, however, she did not have the research background for the necessary close review

Only one panelist had a clear affiliation with a divergent kind of reading instruction.

of dense, detailed, and often abstruse empirical research. Perhaps the inclusion of this panelist was what Alexander had in mind when he spoke about diversity.

In all, there was one middle school teacher on the Panel and although some of the researchers had been teachers, they had not taught for many years. The reading researchers who did spend time in classrooms concentrated on their own special research interests rather than on a broad scope of instructional topics. These researchers did what other researchers do: they pursued their interests. However, for a panel charged with making instructional recommendations to the nation, the limited inquiry of their research contributed to substantial limitations for dealing with the complex practices and needs in classroom reading instruction.

Joanne Yatvin, the principal and former teacher just described, later pointed out that the congressional charge called for a panel that included "leading scientists in reading research, representatives of colleges of education, reading teachers, education administrators and parents." But there were no reading teachers, Yatvin argues, "in the sense" she believed "Congress had intended." Soon after the first meeting, educational psychologist Robert Glaser resigned from the Panel. Yatvin suggested replacing him with a "primary level teacher of reading," but "at the second meeting," she explains, "the Panel chair announced that 'after considerable discussion we concluded that at this stage in the game we might just as well not replace him.'" Yatvin states that the explanation was hardly credible because "the Panel was not told who the 'we' were who made the decision"—the Panel itself had never voted on the decision—and its work "had scarcely begun."[3]

With the Panel in place, work began on the congressional charge, which asked the Panel "to assess the status of research-based knowledge, including the effectiveness of various approaches to teaching children to read."[4]

A close reading of this request shows that the charge left open how this assessment would be made. Given this latitude, a logical start could have been for the Panel, first, to choose to categorize the prominent topics in the field of reading instruction and, second, to examine the research associated with these topics. Had the Panel proceeded in this way, its point of departure would have been the field itself—the topics that reading educators themselves thought were most critical in reading education. Instead, the Panel's point of departure was a set of judgments about "various approaches" that the reading researchers thought critical.

At the Panel's first meeting, in April 1998, a "troubling fact" became apparent to Yatvin: "All the scientist members held the same general view of the reading process." She documents how, "without debate," the Panel accepted a "hierarchy-of-skills model" of learning to read (the model I described in the previous chapter). At this meeting, the Panel identified five areas of reading to be evaluated—phonemic awareness, phonics, fluency, comprehension, and computer technology—and formed a subcommittee for each. Ignored was another legitimate model of reading, Yatvin explains, "a holistic or constructivist view" in which readers do "many things at once, right from the beginning," such as identifying "words by visual memory," matching "sounds to letters," pulling "word meanings from context," understanding "sentences as complete structures," and obtaining "information from content." Also ignored, Yatvin continues, were alternative topics such as "how children's knowledge of oral language, literature and its conventions, and the world apart from print affects their ability to learn to read" and how the "types, quality, or amounts of material children read" affect reading. But with the scientist members dominating, and "with no powerful voices from other philosophical camps on the Panel," Yatvin laments, "it was easy for the majority to believe that theirs [the scientists] was the only legitimate view."[5]

> *"Without debate," the Panel accepted a "hierarchy-of-skills model" of reading.*

"Learning from the Many Voices"

At its first meeting, despite having already selected a model of reading and the topics it would investigate, the Panel discussed plans for a series of regional meetings, which, "panel members agreed," were important for "listening to and learning from the many voices and perspectives of parents, educators, community members and civic or business leaders."[6]

When the Panel next met, on July 24, these regional meetings had been held in Chicago; Portland, Oregon; Houston; New York; and Jackson, Mississippi. And the Panel had heard many voices. They had heard Kathryn Ransom of the International Reading

Association urge considering "that no single approach to reading instruction will work equally well for all children." Several teachers had asked the Panel to appraise Reading Recovery, an early reading intervention program. The Panel had listened and listened and apparently learned that it should continue working on those topics it had selected three months earlier.

Duane Alexander, director of the NICHD, began the July meeting by telling the Panel that "much of what" the members had "heard during the regional meetings went well beyond the charge from Congress" and that "panelists must remember that their responsibility is to 'assess the status of research-based knowledge.'"

According to the minutes of this second meeting, the regional meetings were "successful," and the Panel expressed pleasure because these "meetings highlighted the public's eagerness to receive the Panel's findings." Perhaps hearing of this eagerness inspired the Panel to move quickly forward, spending little if any additional time discussing the actual testimony and its possible applications to the Panel's goals. The absence of this discussion might lead one to conclude that the Panel (or most of the Panel) shared Alexander's view that the regional meetings did not contain much of relevance to the congressional charge itself. This interpretation is strengthened by the reports presented by the five subgroups that had been formed at the previous meeting and that simply continued to guide the Panel's direction.[7]

> *Coincidentally, the Panel's "topics for intensive study" were exactly the same after the regional meetings as before.*

The NRP Report states that "following the regional hearings the panel considered, discussed, and debated several dozen possible topic areas and then settled on the following topics for intensive study": phonemic awareness, phonics, fluency, comprehension, and computer technology.[8] The report fails to acknowledge the coincidence that the topics for intensive study were exactly the same after the regional meetings as they had been before.

Building and Using a Knowledge Base

It is beyond the scope of this book to quote the testimony at the regional meetings that, contrary to Alexander's appraisal, was directly related to "the charge from Congress." I will, however, quote at some length from the testimony of Jan Lewis, a researcher at Pacific Lutheran University, given at the June 1998 regional meeting in Portland, Oregon, in order to provide the reader with a sense of the Panel's objectivity and openness. Not only was the testimony directly related to the charge, but it was a discussion of research-based knowledge derived from a published, annotated database Lewis had coauthored.

Lewis' remarks drew primarily on two works: *Building a Knowledge Base in Reading,* written with Jane Braunger,[9] summarizing numerous research studies related to critical factors in learning to read, and the nearly completed *Using the Knowledge Base in Reading,*[10] describing the application of this research in the classroom. Lewis asked the Panel to consider studying reading instruction from three perspectives. One concerned the importance of "the child's perspective (how they view the world, and how their background experiences help them to make sense of new information within the context of existing information)."

> Current research in learning shows that children understand the world around them in ways based upon their previous experiences. They are developmentally and experientially different from adults. As we are designing instructional experiences for children, particularly young children, we must be careful to provide opportunities for children to make connections to their previous knowledge and experiences, and to understand the purposes of such tasks as they relate to their own lives. Understanding this nature of learning, and the critical role of the interaction between background knowledge and current experience to learning, is basic to any discussion of how children learn to read.

Lewis then summarized sections of *Building a Knowledge Base in Reading* that dealt with some of the research on this topic.

The second perspective concerned the many aspects of children's cognition and lives affecting learning that teachers needed to know. Teachers had to

> make decisions as to how each child best learns, and what is appropriate as a next step. There are many ways to observe and assess a child's learning, and teachers must be aware of a variety of methods and techniques for doing this. But it is also the personal knowledge of the child—the home background, the learning preferences, the background knowledge, the cultural expectations, the

daily experiences of that child—that are as critical to helping each child to reach their potential. Assessment—both informal and formal—must inform teaching decisions. We must move beyond traditional types of standardized tests to include performance based assessments that show learners' development over time. This aspect of observation and assessment must be highlighted by the panel.

Lewis' third perspective for the Panel to examine were studies of exemplary teaching, such as that found in the research she and Braunger had done:

> Continually throughout our most recent investigations, we have heard teachers talk about a "balance" in their instruction. These teachers provide print rich environments: libraries of books, child-made books, posters, signs, and other artifacts; centers with a wide variety of writing materials; areas for reading, talking, drawing, and sharing. They provide children with a wide variety of strategies for reading words and creating meaning from those words; these teachers understand there is much more to reading than "decoding" and "comprehending." Strategies focus on a wide variety of ways to look at word structures and patterns, the role of context in providing confirmation to problem solving of unknown words, and involve an understanding of the alphabetic principle. For these teachers, reading is a problem solving process and they provide a wide range of strategies to support children as they develop in their reading. Comprehending text becomes thinking critically about the story, its structure, its information, and its contribution to a reader's own experiences. Instruction occurs in a wide variety of ways: some focused, some explicit, some directed, some evolutionary, some implicit; to the whole group, to a small group, to one child . . . but, it is all based upon the teacher's understanding of where learners are in their development, what they need in their development, and how to best involve the children.

Lewis then candidly addressed the research perspectives she thought dominated the NRP:

> I find a perspective based in educational anthropology to be missing from the [panel's perspective]. Finally, after years of debate within its own community, educational researchers have come to accept the validity, reliability, and critical importance of qualitative research to the "big picture" of coming to understand the processes of teaching and learning. Qualitative research provides the context and perspec-

tive to help us best interpret how theories and philosophies actually work within the reality of our everyday lives. I urge the panel to acknowledge, accept, and interweave this research into their findings.

Lewis worried about educational researchers who "talk about the research, the answers."

Lewis concluded that she worried "when we, as educational and research communities, begin to talk of *the* way to teach, *the* research to consider, and that we finally have *the* answers."[11]

"What Is Really Happening"?

Despite testimony like this, which provided deep and broad insights into teaching and learning, the Panel was not persuaded to alter its course. By the third meeting, on September 10, 1998, the Panel was focused on the progress the subcommittees were making. The Alphabetics Subgroup, for example, reported that it had now "interpreted its task as identifying a claim about the important alphabetic process in learning to read." That "alphabetic process" was phonemic awareness—the ability to focus on the smallest units of sound in words—because there was "evidence that phonemic awareness is one of the best predictors (the second being letter-name knowledge) of how well children will learn to read."[12]

Two months later, at the November 9, 1998, meeting, the Panel appeared to be having some second thoughts about the topics it had chosen to investigate and those it had ignored, such as home and preschool influences, "what is really happening in classrooms," writing instruction, and the use of worksheets. Pausing for a critical self-appraisal, the Panel identified twelve additional areas it thought most important and discussed the possibility of including them within the subcommittee work. Had these areas been included, the Panel might have undertaken a more substantial appraisal of reading instruction. The Panel rejected its own proposal, however. Inexplicably, little more was said about these topics in the following meetings, little work on them seems to have been done, and they soon dropped out of sight as the Panel continued to hone the preferred five topics.[13]

The majority of the Panel had little interest in what reading teachers had to say.

"Real-Life Classroom Issues"

As the composition of the Panel and Joanne Yatvin's failed effort suggest, the majority of members had little interest in considering what reading teachers had to say about reading instruction. Had the panel members had such an interest, they readily could have informed themselves in several ways, such as surveying educational journals for articles on teachers' views on "questions relevant to reading instruction."

Around the time the formation of the Panel was announced, for example, an article in the *Reading Teacher* reported the results of a survey of U.S. elementary classroom teachers' instructional beliefs and practices. The crucial "real-life classroom issues" for these teachers were not whether or how to teach phonics and other word skills—the survey showed that the majority of teachers already did so! Rather, their key issues included

- how to accommodate the incredible range of students' needs and reading levels
- how to deal with the frustration of not enough time to teach
- how to teach well with "insufficient quality materials"
- how to accommodate large classes of diverse learners[14]

We can see how this survey of important issues not only puts into serious question a national panel having to inform teachers that they should teach "skills" but also underlines the ill-advised and inevitably sterile method of abstracting aspects of written language learning from real-life teaching in real-life classrooms.

In addition to surveys, the Panel could have used other means to obtain teachers' views, such as contacting Internet educational discussion groups (listservs). With the real-life classroom issues of the survey just discussed in mind, I did exactly that, posting a query to teachers on the Teachers Applying Whole Language listserv, a discussion group that has a broad range of participants, from seasoned teachers to graduate students, from teachers well-versed in whole language teaching to others who want to learn what it is. Because it is an open listserv, it also has participants who are antagonistic to whole language teaching. I was especially interested in obtaining this group's views, particularly from those teachers who used a whole language approach, because the advocates of scientific reading instruction often characterize whole language teachers as those who eschew skills instruction.

I asked, "What are the primary two or three issues/factors that you think are most important for teaching reading?" The predominant answers were as follows:

- Teaching to each child's individual needs. Knowing how to support each child's reading growth in the unique manner required. Understanding where students are in their learning process when they come to the classroom and focusing on their development/progress rather than on how they compare to a norm.
- Ongoing assessment of each child's reading progress and areas of reading difficulty to plan for his or her work in reading.
- Having a large variety of wonderful books, both fiction and nonfiction, at many different levels (lots of levels, genres, authors; and multiple copies of many of the titles), that engage students and relate to their own lives.
- Encouraging students to think about the way reading relates to their lives and experiences.
- Including skills within a broad tapestry of reading.
- Having students engage in lots of writing for many real purposes.
- Using shared reading, reading aloud, guided reading, word study, reading conferences, mini-lessons, independent reading, talking about books, shared writing, independent writing, and so on.
- Social/psychological/economic support for children and their families who are faced with difficulties in these areas.
- Strong home-school links and evening or afternoon meetings for parents to help them learn what we know about reading.
- Longer blocks of uninterrupted time for literacy instruction (extremely difficult to accomplish in a large school where playground, lunchroom, and special area teachers must be tightly scheduled).
- A class size that allows the teacher to know each student as a reader. Reasonable class size (twelve to eighteen for beginning readers).

The view of reading instruction expressed here, while duplicating the predominant findings of the national survey published in the

Reading Teacher, is also richer. These teachers were concerned with the wide variation in students' reading knowledge and needs, but when talking about individual needs, these teachers were not referring only to children with reading problems; they saw all children in their classrooms as having individual needs, such as special interests that motivate them or creative writing talents. The teachers' concern with having many books in the classroom expressed awareness of the contribution extensive reading makes in children's reading acquisition: reinforcing skills, words, vocabulary, concepts, and reading strategies the children have learned; deepening comprehension; gaining experiences with reading various kinds of nonfiction and fiction; and encouraging an enthusiasm for reading. Again, taking cues from teachers, the Panel could have addressed many permutations of the benefits of extensive reading.

The responses also focused on writing and indicated the teachers' awareness that, as youngsters hear, distinguish, and manipulate sounds associated with letters they write, and attempt to represent words through strings of letters that contain the sounds associated with the words, writing contributes to phonemic awareness and phonics knowledge. The teachers also recognized that when learners write stories that can be read to teachers and classmates, they simultaneously learn plot lines, character portrayal, and many other aspects vital to reading development. Incredibly, the importance that these and other teachers have given to writing and its role in reading development did not find its way into the range of topics of primary concern to the NRP.

> The Panel should have examined the conditions that affect instruction, not just instructional methods.

The inclusion of class size on the list jibes with the considerable research documenting the contribution of class size to children's reading achievement. This research should have been essential in the NRP's work because at its base is the fact that instruction in beginning reading is not only a matter of whether teachers have particular competencies but also a matter of whether they have the opportunity to use those competencies. When we look at the Panel's charge to study "specific questions relevant to reading development and reading disabilities and for informing specific instructional decisions," we see that the Panel should not have focused exclusively on instructional methods; it should also have examined the conditions that affect instruction and allow sound instruction to blossom. In the class-size research, it was found that the most "effective teachers," those whose students ranked in the top 15 percent of achievement gains in reading, had many qualities that were not extraordinary. They monitored student learning progress; when children did not learn, they used alternative strategies in reteaching; they had high expectations for student learning; they were enthusiastic; they had a sense of humor that promoted learning; they had a love of children; they used a broad range of resources and activities; and they had excellent personal interactions with their students.[15] But, of the fifty effective teachers studied, only three had large classes.

"None of the Stilted, Choppy Reading"

While reading the answers to my question on the listserv poll, I noticed a decided lack of emphasis on teaching phonemic and phonetic skills and asked the respondents about it. The following amplifications from two teachers are representative of the replies and the thinking about the complexities of teaching (other replies can be found in the Appendix).

One teacher, Ruby Clayton, wrote: "I am in my twenty-seventh year of teaching. I have taught kindergartners to read by sounding out words, but comprehension was always secondary. Back then, we did a lot of work with letters-sounds. My first reading strategy for them was 'sound out' the word. I thought if kids could read the words they would comprehend the story.

"Writing consisted of having them 'write' nursery rhymes they had memorized. My main purpose was to free them from having to think about what to write so they could use their skill of sounding out words. Almost daily, I'd give auditory drills where I'd say the sound and children would write the letter or letters that made the sound. Children would take mock 'spelling tests' so I could see how many sounds they could get down. So, although we did a lot of 'practice' work to get them ready for reading and writing, not much real reading and writing took place.

"Over the past few years, I have been emphasizing meaning and I have seen that the children *love* reading real books. They fight over them. Some children have almost taught themselves to read. They push books into my hand, demanding that I read this one next. They take every bit of paper I can give them so they can write what they want. And this year, all of my first graders in my k/1 multiage class are readers. They *know* that the reading must make sense, and automatically self-correct when it doesn't. Their reading *sounds* like reading should, with proper voice tone and inflection, with none of the stilted, choppy reading that I had before. And most important, the kids don't think reading is hard work. They don't know what a basal [reading textbook program] is, and think library books are gold.

"I still teach phonological awareness and phonics in a very short five- to ten-minute drill that involves the letter, hand motions, and a picture that represents the sound. I also do rhyming word drills, that is, 'Give me a word that rhymes with _____.' And the kids say 'chair, bear' and so on. Sometimes we sing a song that involves saying a word and its beginning sound—'baby, baby, /b/ /b/ /b/.' I include these 'exercises' because this way the kids seem to catch on easily, without pressure. And I don't have to use worksheets to see if they hear the sounds or know the corresponding letters.

"The kids learn the letters and sounds because they are using them for real purposes. When I periodically assess the kids, the letters, sounds, words that each knows at any particular time are always unique to the child, so it would be ludicrous for me to try to teach them all the same thing. I now tailor my teaching to the needs of the child and use no program to tell me what the child needs."

The "Reading Fairy" Passed Over Them

Another teacher, Anita Britton, replied: "I see phonics instruction as one skill students need to support them in reading. I teach some phonics skills with spelling in writing workshop lessons. I teach it in response to what my students are doing and want to know, in balance and with appropriate context.

"Further, by the time children reach third and fourth grade, the focus on phonics becomes a real detriment. Those students who had once loved reading and listening to stories as preschoolers (as reported to me by their parents during conferences) wind up hating reading and feeling that somehow the 'reading fairy' has passed over them. I have found that some struggling readers started to love reading again in third and fourth grades if they were honored as learners learning the way that fit them best and not drilled to 'sound it out.'

"One inventory I do with my 'struggling' students at the beginning of each year gives me information about my students' reading strategies. It asks questions such as 'When you come to a word you don't know, what do you do?' and 'Do you consider yourself a good reader? Why or why not?' My struggling readers predominantly think that good readers are people who 'can sound out long words.' When I press them for other strategies, they often have none. This tells me that they either haven't been taught other strategies— syntactic and semantic strategies (reading on, predicting and confirming, etc.)—or have let those strategies go after the 'experts' have given them the message that the only way to learn a new word is to 'sound it out.'

"I believe that students are honored as learners when they read books at their level of independence and interest, as they do in 'Reading Workshop.' When I introduce 'Reading Workshop,' you should see the looks on their faces when they realize they will be choosing the book they want to read and receive support from everyone in our room whenever they need it.

"The 'Books I've Read' list, which my children keep in their portfolios, tells me a great deal. At the beginning of the year, few books are listed and many of those books are fairly 'safe' (books that students have heard over and over, have few new words, are repetitive, etc.). Within the first month of 'Reading Workshop,' these students read more challenging books. They start sharing interesting or funny parts with other students in class, asking other students about words they don't know (at the beginning of the year, they are embarrassed to do this, skip over the word to avoid the embarrassment, and consequently, have little comprehension). During read-aloud time, these students move from little participation in the conversation to active and anticipatory interaction with books."

I see stark differences in the views of the NRP and those of reading teachers.

"Broad Questions"

I see stark differences in the views of the NRP and the reading teachers' own comments. The NRP's mechanical, restricted conception of reading, which the Report describes as "broad questions," was formulated by researchers who do quantitative experiments that identify a few variables of written language acquisition from the complex elements and interactions that actually constitute teaching and learning to read.[16] These researchers then proceed on the assumption that the complex elements and interactions are ancillary to the variables that determine reading success or failure. The NRP demonstrated no interest in undertaking an extensive examination of what teachers actually do in actual classrooms with a couple of dozen or more actual children with different written language competencies, different motivations, different family experiences, different personalities, different levels of confidence, and so on. Nor did the NRP have any interest in pursing the differences between literacy, a process that includes *both* reading and writing, and reading alone.

The teachers' listserv replies, like those in the national survey of teachers' views in the *Reading Teacher*, underscore the question of whether the importance of teaching alphabetic skills should have been the chief issue in a response to the congressional charge, since all the teachers saw skills instruction as an essential part of both what they do and of the learning-to-read process! The teachers were not simply concerned with teaching skills as needed, that is, teaching a skill once they had identified a student's need to know that skill. Rather, the teachers aimed to teach a skill when the learning was most meaningful, that is, when children saw the value of using the skill to master written language. In addition to skills, the teachers were also concerned with helping students develop an array of strategies for identifying words and gaining meaning from text.

The teachers in my poll were also concerned that putting an excessive emphasis on word skills might result in beginning readers not achieving competence in a variety of additional strategies for reading, strategies especially necessary for high-level material in later grades. An excessive skills emphasis that encourages children to see reading as word work rather than as an experience that informs and excites them and fires their imagination (again, a processes within which skills contribute) could discourage enthusiasm for reading and thereby encourage aliteracy, that is, students who know how to read but have no interest in reading.

The teachers saw the necessity of using children's interests and motivations in formulating the literacy curriculum. They expressed specific concern with the affective side of learning—children's motivation, interests, joys, love, desires, needs—as critical in learning to read and in the creation of lifelong readers.

They were focused on knowing, through ongoing assessment, what children needed to be taught as their reading progressed. Attention to the many different ways children learn and their different strengths and needs was key to the teachers, who also recognized they had to be competent in the use of different teaching approaches. Ongoing assessment meant not tests, but professionally informed observations of children's reading.

The teachers were also aware that children learn within a classroom community that includes—or should include—many learning interactions, such as sharing reading, mutual help with reading, talking about and recommending books, and more. For these teachers, community activities were integral to literacy acquisition, not simply add-ons.

Not a single beginning reading teacher was on the Panel.

Unfortunately, the absence of even a single beginning reading teacher on the Panel and the reading researchers' lack of interest in (and perhaps unfamiliarity with) complex beginning reading classroom teaching facilitated the National Reading Panel's fixation on the decontextualized parts of reading instruction it described as broad questions. It is these decontexualized parts that fill the NRP Report, to which we now turn.

3️⃣ Training and Other Kinds of "Boosts"

100,000 Studies

Following the publication of the NRP Report, the figure of 100,000 studies, frequently and variously repeated, quickly took on an unquestioned life and legitimacy of its own. Perhaps all those who repeated the figure dared not tamper with a formidable sum that attributed a potent scholarship to the Report (a term I will now use, instead of NRP Report, to simplify the prose). The number of studies the Panel actually used for its report, however, was a far distance from 100,000. Some have said that the actual number was small because the Panel could not find many studies of sufficient scientific merit. Physicist Harry Lipkin, for example, stated, "Any respected national panel called upon to review 100,000 published research studies must first clear away all the useless garbage and focus on the comparatively small number of useful, correct and relevant studies. That only a few hundred studies fit this criterion is par for the course."[1] The following description of the studies selected by the Panel will reveal whether this was so or whether something besides science matched the studies finally selected with the topics dear to the hearts of most of the panelists.

The first database the Panel used did contain about 100,000 published studies on reading, going back to 1966. From this number, the Panel began to prune, using several criteria: A first pruning eliminated all studies that were not about reading development from preschool through high school; studies on literacy skills needed in occupations or studies on brain functioning and reading, for example, were eliminated. Another pruning summarily removed studies that were about key aspects of reading development such as motivation and reading, writing and reading, and children's interests and reading, which the majority of the Panel showed no interest in examining. In other words, the Panel's arbitrary and a priori conclusions, as discussed in the previous chapter, provided the overarching pruning device for removing the scientific knowledge that should have informed the Panel's inquiry.

> *The Panel's arbitrary and a priori conclusions provided the pruning device for culling the 100,000 studies.*

The number of studies was further reduced by the Panel's definition of scientific research, which was limited to quantitative, experimental studies, the kind that have a research and a control group, quantitative outcomes, and statistical analyses. Excluded, with few exceptions, were other kinds of research, such as qualitative studies (that is, systematic observations of classroom literacy activities), which can be invaluably insightful and instructive and are also widely regarded as legitimately scientific in the professional literature.

Another pruning step was based on the extent to which the published paper on the study adequately described the subjects, instruction used, outcome measures, data, statistical analyses, and other basic aspects of the research. Presumably, if a study fulfilled these criteria, it passed muster for minimum scientific soundness. Although these gauges are valid, in this and the following chapters I will address the question of whether they are sufficient for judging the scientific soundness of the studies.

> *After the pruning, there remained 52 studies on phonemic awareness, 38 on phonics, 14 on silent reading.*

When the culling was completed, there remained 52 studies on phonemic awareness (the ability to separate and manipulate speech sounds mentally and orally, as when blending or separating phonemes in order to identify words); 38 studies on phonics; 14 on silent reading; and 203 on sixteen categories of comprehension instruction, that is, about 12 or 13 studies on average in each category. Certainly these numbers might be sufficient for drawing some modest, reasonable conclusions. However, even before we delve into their quality, it is reasonable to propose that they are grossly insufficient for establishing national legislative policy based on claims about scientific imperatives.

The Meta-Analysis

For the "Alphabetics" (phonemic awareness and phonics) sections of the Report, the NRP evaluated the research with a meta-analysis, a statistical method that pools a group of studies and estimates the extent of an effect—large, medium, small, or absent—that something has on something else. In this case, the meta-analysis estimated the effect sizes of aspects of instruction on achievement. Effect sizes and a meta-analysis can provide useful information but can also have substantial deficiencies, such as the well-known GIGO problem of "garbage in, garbage out," a term for underscoring the inability of a broad statistical analysis to exceed the caliber of the studies used.

> *The meta-analysis did not eliminate the GIGO (garbage in, garbage out) problem.*

Reexamining the Report's meta-analysis and effect size calculations on their own statistical ground is important in appraising the Report's validity, and such reexaminations have already documented considerable deficiencies.[2] However, beneath the statistical calculations are even deeper problems, which themselves undermine the effect size calculations and meta-analysis. Shrouded in the plethora of calculations are the failure of the studies to prove what the Report concludes they prove and, even worse, the Report's frequently misleading interpretations of the studies. These conclusions will be explained and supported by a close examination of the individual studies themselves, beginning with an examination of the NRP's appraisal of the contribution phonemic awareness makes in learning to read.

"My Focus Is on Reading Words"

An examination of the studies should not proceed without first positing the question, What is reading? Throughout the Report the term is used liberally, but its definition is ever-changing. Reading in one place might mean reading real or nonsense words and somewhere else mean reading aloud smoothly and rapidly. Seldom does it mean comprehending text, a process most people would define as key in reading. As Joanne Yatvin observed:

> In the various sub-committee reports "reading" is used to represent many different kinds of operations, from accurate pronunciation of nonsense words to a thorough understanding of a written text. When a sub-committee report asserts that a particular instructional technique "improves children's reading," the public deserves to know whether the authors mean word calling, speed, smoothness, literal comprehension or the ability to assimilate a subtle and complex set of ideas.[3]

The Report's predominant definition of reading is reading at the word level, with a special stress on decoding skills, a definition explained and supported with citations of publications by panelist

> *In the NRP Report, seldom does "reading" mean comprehending text.*

Linnea Ehri. Summarizing these publications, the Report explains, "research on word reading processes has distinguished several ways to read words." A reader might identify a word "from memory, sometimes called sight word reading," or, if encountering a word "never read before," could transform "graphemes into phonemes" and then "blend the phonemes to form" a word with a "recognizable meaning." Or, the reader might use "analogy to known words."[4] A reader's use of context, syntax, and other written language information gleaned from a sentence or the broader text containing the word is noticeably absent from the Report's explanation. As if to justify the definition, the Report cites Ehri's publications in which she explains that her "focus is on how readers develop skill at reading words by alphabetic processing," but not on how readers use "contextual" information (textual meaning, syntax, etc.) for identifying words.[5] Not readily apparent to readers of the Report who are not reading specialists is that Ehri's model of learning to read and of reading words *out of meaningful textual contexts* is simply that—a model, one among several, and hardly established fact.

> The predominant definition of reading in the Report is reading at the word level, with a stress on decoding skills.

The fact that what guides both Ehri and the Report is a theoretical model is clear in the title of the edited volume *Theoretical Models and Processes of Reading*, a collection containing one of her essays. Also included in this volume are models that run counter to Ehri's, such as the one detailed in an essay by Yetta and Kenneth Goodman. In the Goodman model, "as readers make use of their knowledge of all the language [information], they predict, make inferences, select significant features, confirm, and constantly work toward constructing meaningful text. Not only are they constructing meaning, they are constructing themselves as readers."[6]

> The Report's word-level model of reading is based on a theory; it is not a scientific fact.

The Report does not explain that its chosen model of decontextualized word-level reading is based on a theory; rather, it implies that it is a scientific fact. Given this assertion, the Report also leaves unaddressed the effect of this *theory* on the ultimate validity of both the Report's conclusions and the Panel's final advice.

In this chapter and the next, I will review in detail most of the fifty-two studies in the meta-analysis on phonemic awareness (PA). In order to minimize tedium, I will not review the remaining studies because these either further illustrate research problems I will have already amply discussed, are older studies of little contemporary value, or are a researcher's additional publications essentially duplicating what I will have already examined. Reviewing these remaining studies would strengthen my critique but not add to its scope. Although most of the studies I critique are in this and the following chapters, after providing what I felt was sufficient evidence for my evaluation, I put the reviews of a few other studies in the Appendix.

Compared with What?

Imagine an experiment in which a control group of first graders is instructed in muffin making and compared with an experimental group trained in phonemic awareness skills. At the end of the training period, reading tests show that the experimental group did better, leading the experimenters to conclude that the study demonstrates the superiority of phonemic awareness training in beginning reading. Later, the National Reading Panel calculates the effect size and reports it as large. Had this actually happened, the preposterous conclusions would be evident to any reader. Yet the kind of incongruous comparison I have described is exactly what is contained in many of the studies used in the Report. I call this a "compared with what?" problem, that is, studies using control groups that provide no proper contrast for judging the value of the instruction used by the experimental group.

> *The "compared with what?" problem runs through many of the studies cited in the Report, making them meaningless.*

A second kind of "compared with what?" problem is based on the kind of classroom reading instruction that benefits from the addition of a PA training program. If, for example, both an experimental and a control group were taught with a long-discredited classroom reading program, and the experimental group were to benefit from additional instruction in a phonemic awareness program, the comparison would merely show that phonemic awareness training can assist children using a bad reading program and not that phonemic awareness training necessarily needs to be attached to all reading programs. Nonetheless, this second "compared with what?" problem characterizes the experimental designs of many studies used in the Report.

Skills and the "Valuable Metacognitive Component"

Both "compared with what?" problems are in a study by reading researcher Anne Cunningham, in which kindergarten and first-grade students were placed either in one of two skills-training groups or in a control group. One of the training groups learned to blend phonemes (e.g., What word do you get when you blend the sounds /b/, /a/, /t/ together?) and to segment them in words. In a summary of the study, the Report explains that the other skills-training group learned these skills plus "metacognitive activities that included . . . observing and practicing how to use" the skills in reading. The control group, however, just listened to stories. The results showed, explains the Report, "that at the end of [the training period], the two [skills] treatment groups outperformed the control group on measures of [phonemic awareness] and reading in both grades." Between the two training groups, the one trained in metacognitive activities, the Report continues, "achieved higher reading scores."[7]

The first "compared with what?" problem is in the experimental-control comparison that pitted sound and word instruction against no instruction (that is, just listening to a story and answering questions about it). Consequently, making such a statistical comparison and concluding that instruction had a greater effect on phonemic awareness and reading is not especially informative.

The first-grade classroom instruction used a "basal reading series" (a set of readers and accompanying materials organized sequentially, usually by grade level) "that emphasized phonics, word recognition, and reading comprehension"[8]—important information not mentioned in the Report, and the root of the second "compared with what?" problem.

Because this reading program was not sufficient instruction for all beginning readers and the study did not include a different kind of regular classroom instruction, the Report cannot maintain, as it does, that the study shows, in some general way, that special and separate skills training will benefit a beginning reading program. The most we can conclude is that in beginning reading instruction, if a basal program like this one is used, adding a phonemic skills training could help mollify the program's deficiencies.

Commenting on the "metacognitive component" used in one of the training groups (again, "observing and practicing" the skills), the Report notes that this component "may be valuable in providing a bridge between phonological awareness skills and reading processes." Left with this conclusion, a reader might assume that this might be a winning recipe for promoting reading. However, the original study explains that metacognitive activities meant that students were encouraged to identify unknown words in several ways, including the use of *both* letter sounds and context—that is, the use of *semantic information* to see if the word they were trying to identify made sense within the meaning of the text.

This combination of strategies is quite different from a focus on letter sounds alone, but nothing in the Report's description of the study hints at the children's use of context information to identify words. To have done so would, of course, have raised questions about the actual strategies that advanced reading and the meaning of the effect calculations. This is the first of many of the Report's misrepresentations of studies that I will discuss.

How to Demonstrate a "Training Boost"

The Report cites a number of studies supposedly demonstrating that phonemic awareness "training boosts children's reading and spelling performance" and describes several of them. In one such boosting study, by Benita Blachman and her colleagues, "low-income, inner-city kindergartners" were given phonemic awareness training for eleven weeks, and at end of the program, the Report states, the training group "outperformed controls on PA tasks . . . and training transferred to reading."[9]

Omitted in the Report's explanation of the "boost" are the differences in both the curriculum and the teacher-student ratios. While the training children met in groups of *four or five*, the control group had *"whole class instruction"*; while the training group engaged in a variety of phonemic awareness activities and games that included learning to read real words, the control group's only written language education was learning "letter names and sounds."[10] Given these differences, there's little wonder that outcome differences were found on tests of phonemic awareness and reading word lists (the definition of reading not mentioned in the Report).

"Boosts Reading Performance"?

Also described as demonstrating that phonemic awareness training "boosts children's reading and spelling performance"[11] was a study by Norwegian educator Albert Lie. Contrary to this description, however, for reading performance the study actually showed the opposite of the Report's claim!

> *A Norwegian study actually shows the opposite of what is claimed in the Report.*

First graders in the training program were compared with children taught to read by the "usual method" in Norway, which from the scant description in the published paper appears to be a phonics approach that teaches associations between sounds and letters, blending sounds, and so on.

Possibly the NRP drew its conclusion about a PA "boost" from the reading test results at the end of the first year. But then there was the end of second grade, and the Report does not tell readers, nor is it evident in the meta-analysis, what the researcher found and concluded at that time: "the differences between the experimental groups and the control group in reading were significant at the end of Grade 1, but not at the end of Grade 2."[12]

With respect to the spelling, we again have to consider "compared with what?" At the same time that the Report lauds this "boost," it ignores the question of whether a heavy skills curriculum, such as that used in Norway, is the best beginning instruction for spelling. We cannot conclude—and the effect size calculations cannot demonstrate—that because the training programs improved the spelling of children taught with the usual Norwegian method, the training program is necessary for beginning reading instruction.

"Boosts Reading and Spelling"?

Another "boost" study was done in Sweden with kindergartners, comparing a phonemic training group with a control group whose education consisted of "a fairly low degree of structure and a pronounced emphasis on social and aesthetic development in playful settings" and no literacy education.[13]

The follow-up to another "boost" study showed no training benefit in tests of silent reading, spelling, and reading nonsense words.

At the end of six to eight weeks of training, there seemed to be a boost for some children but not the majority. Researchers Ake Olofsson and Ingvar Lundberg report, "the distribution of scores on the reading test [shows that] about one fifth of the children seem to have some reading ability, while more than half of them cannot read at all."[14] More revealing about the "boost" is a follow-up study of the children at the end of first grade: although the students in the phonemic training program did better on phonemic awareness tasks, there were no group differences for silent reading, spelling, and reading nonsense words.[15]

"No Blending Instruction"

How can a three-week study with kindergartners limited only to blending sounds provide useful information for beginning reading instruction? Apparently the NRP thought it could and included it in its pool of PA studies. One group of kindergartners ("prereaders") was trained to listen to and blend sound patterns ("k——ep, what word is that?"). Another group learned to blend words and pseudo-words shown on cards ("This is the word *feef*. If I put this letter /k/ over the first letter, what does it say?" [*keef*]). The control group, in contrast, was given "no blending instruction" in words and pseudo-words. Instead, they practiced "sound-letter correspondences daily, using games and other activities."[16]

Of course the students who were given no blending instruction did worse on a blending test at the end of three weeks. Of potential value was the finding that the children who learned blending with the visual aids did best on the blending test. Beyond this, the study does not demonstrate the benefit of these blending exercises on reading acquisition and has no place in a national report on reading instruction.

A "Highly Effective" Program

"Highly effective at teaching decoding skill to disabled readers" compared with the "untreated controls"[17] is the Report's description of the outcome of PA training in a study by Joanna Williams.

Omitted from the Report's summary—and apparently not considered pertinent in appraising effect size—is any information about the students and the instructional curriculum. The paper itself explains that the "learning disabled" children, in special education classrooms in New York City, were taught with "reading instruction [in 1975 that] might best be described as eclectic. Teachers used a different basal-reading program in almost every classroom; only one series was used by three teachers, and two other series were used by two teachers each. About 75% of the teachers also used phonics materials (sometimes the phonic component of the basal series and sometimes a separate phonics program was used)." Worksheets too were part of the curriculum.[18]

What we have, in other words, are special education classes that appear to be doing nothing "special": traditional, conventional reading programs that included phonics instruction—programs that perhaps contributed to the students' reading problems in the first place—predominated. We could conclude that the training was a helpful adjunct to conventional basal reading programs used in conventional special education classes in 1975. Not exactly a persuasive demonstration of a "highly effective" and successful program.

"Helps Them Learn to Read"

The Report considers a study coauthored by NRP member Linnea Ehri[19] as one whose "findings indicate that teaching children to segment and spell helps them learn to read as well as spell words."[20]

While the kindergartners in the training group were taught to spell by dividing and stringing letter sounds in lists of words, the control group learned the letter sounds used in the words but was not taught how to divide sounds or to string them for spelling words. And no control group used an alternative way to learn how to spell. On the post-tests, not surprisingly, the training group had better scores on tests of spelling nonsense words, identifying the spelling that matched a spoken word, and learning new words.

We can conclude that children who learn to associate sounds and letters and string them together to spell words will have superior word reading and spelling scores than children who learn only to associate sounds and letters. But, as was the case in studies discussed earlier, with no alternative method for learning to spell and read, this study provides little direction for the best way to teach spelling. Finally, given this study's duration of thirty-six days, and without any long-term follow-up, the Report's conclusion that this research shows that this particular training "helps [children] learn to read and spell" stretches the term *helps*. Presuming that this limited study can contribute to national policy on reading is also a stretch.

"Disappointing Results"

Exactly what "boost" is identified by the Report in a long-term study with kindergartners is not clear when one reads the study itself.

For example, unmentioned in the Report is the conclusion by the researchers, Wolfgang Schneider and his colleagues, that the "long-term training effects . . . yielded disappointing results" because the trained group did not have signifi-

> *Absent in the Report is the researchers' conclusion that "long-term training effects . . . yielded disappointing results."*

cantly superior results over the control group on reading and spelling tests. "Contrary to expectations," explained the researchers, not only were there no group differences on the reading and spelling tests at the end of grade 2, but "the control group tended to outperform the training groups on the reading test," although the differences were not statistically significant.[21]

Perplexed by the failure to achieve the anticipated effects, the researchers did another study, but unlike the previous investigation, this one provided no measure of reading comprehension! On a word identification test, the training group did score better, but here too the researchers were disappointed because "the effect sizes" on the tests "were rather small." For example, out of 140 test words, the training group identified an average of 82.22 and the control group identified 76.99, and "the differences were not reliable."[22] The training group did do somewhat better on a spelling test. Out of 32 words, the group had an average of 19.31 correct, compared with the control's 15.88. Such was the boost in reading and spelling.

"More Success"

It is not clear why a study that compared computer-assisted PA training with teacher-led instruction is included in the Report. After eighteen weeks in first grade, Dutch kindergartners who used a computer program for twelve weeks to learn blending skills had statistically better test results in decoding but not in spelling than had another group that had not used the program in kindergarten. Not much can be concluded from this because the first-grade teachers did not use a uniform method—some regularly emphasized blending, but others did not—thereby making difficult comparisons of the kindergarten training with instruction. None of this deterred the panelists from interpreting this "study with kindergartners in the Netherlands" as one that "reported more success" for blending training.

With respect to the value of computer-assisted instruction, researchers Pieter Reitsma and Ralph Wesseling were disappointed in the results. Their "research findings," they wrote, "do not suggest that computer exercises have more potential or advantages over teacher-led instruction. A fair and valid comparison between computer-assisted versus teacher-led instruction is extremely difficult to make, and one can seriously question the usefulness of such a contrast."[23] Hence, in terms of what the researchers expected to find, they acknowledged that the study had not accomplished this.

"Comparable Gains"

Another "boost" study trained inner-city kindergartners in phonemic awareness and compared them with kindergartners who "followed the usual curriculum which adopted a 'whole language' approach designed to foster interest in literacy."[24]

Where was the boost? Not at the end of kindergarten, when the training group did have better scores on tests of phonemic awareness, but not on reading and spelling tests, where a boost would have really counted. There, reported Susan Brady and her colleagues, the groups showed "comparable gains."[25]

> *The skills-training group and "whole language" group had comparable scores on reading and spelling tests.*

Nor was there a boost at the end of first grade, where the groups' reading achievement scores again were not significantly different.

It is important to note here that this study is an example of research in which students in a program described as whole language attained reading achievement comparable to those in skills training, showing the whole language program to be at least as effective in promoting reading. In the chapters ahead, we will look at other studies that made this comparison.

"The Strong Test of Intervention"

"Reading disabled" kindergartners attending a large, urban school district were also reported to have benefited from a PA boost. By now the reader is likely to anticipate the written language activities (or lack of such activities) of the control counterparts.

Explaining why the training group did better on measures of phonic analysis and reading (defined here as identifying and writing letter names and reading words) requires more than knowing about the unmatched educational experiences between experimental and control groups, however. In this instance, also unmatched were the inservice training and the support of the respective teachers. Those who taught the phonemic training activities participated in inservice sessions spaced throughout the year. Researchers Rollanda O'Connor and her colleagues also observed the teachers either weekly or biweekly and provided modeling of how to teach the training activities. The control group teachers, in contrast, received no comparable inservice training, no oversight of their teaching, and no instructional modeling. We do not know the extent to which this disparate professional training and support contributed to differences in instruction, but it is certainly obvious that the experimental design was not balanced.

Yet even with these imbalances in education and in teacher support favoring the experimental group, there is no evidence that the PA training boost lasted beyond kindergarten and transferred to a fuller definition of reading. The researchers themselves were aware of this problem

> *This study provided no evidence that the PA training boost lasted beyond kindergarten.*

when noting: "Recent articles acknowledge the problems with one-year studies. We improve phonological skills, find effects on low-level reading skills, but the strong test of intervention will be in better acquisition of reading throughout the primary grades for children predicted to fail."[26] Unfortunately, the "strong test of intervention" standard that failed to demonstrate a long-term outcome is not reflected in the Report.

"In the Absence of Direct Evidence"

According to the Report, a short-term study with kindergartners demonstrated a considerable effect size on the reading of kindergartners who learned to segment and blend phonemes. It will not be necessary to appraise the results of the study by Joseph Torgesen and his colleagues,[27] given the statements in a later paper in which Torgesen and other colleagues reported follow-up testing done two and a half years after the study had started. A boost? Yes, the children who had received PA training continued to do better on PA measures, but, no, this superiority "did not produce a corresponding advantage in real word reading" as measured by a test of word identification. The researchers cautioned that they had not "really verified" that phonemic intervention training "will make a permanent and significant difference in long-term reading outcome" and that theirs is not the only research that has failed to obtain a long-term training benefit.[28] PA training programs may "eventually" be shown to have such a benefit, the researchers advised, but "in the absence of direct evidence we simply do not know if this assumption is correct."[29]

The First Step: "Manipulate the Sounds"

The Report's claims that PA training provides a boost in reading acquisition and that "a variety" of such training programs have been "found to be effective," especially for poor children and children "at risk for developing reading problems," have not been supported by the studies reviewed in this chapter.[30] Neither have we seen evidence that "PA training was effective in boosting reading comprehension."[31] Nor have studies reviewed so far shown that the instruction described by the teachers in the previous chapter, in which phonemic awareness is integrated in a comprehensive written language approach, is an inferior teaching approach.

The key issue is not whether children need skills, but how they should be taught.

Beyond not proving these claims, we have seen several instances of the Report's distortion of studies, especially through the omission of key information and conclusions made by the researchers themselves. It should be clear, however, that misuse and erroneous conclusions of research are not the fault of the original investigators. In most instances the researchers were conducting investigations of one small PA issue or another, and the methodological deficiencies of the studies matter a great deal only because, in most instances, these studies have been used by others to make unwarranted national recommendations that have helped justify unwarranted national legislation. It is important to restate that the key instructional issue is not whether children benefit from knowing, separating, and blending sounds in words, but whether this knowledge has to be taught as those proselytizers of scientific reading instruction not only advocate but legislate. The next chapter continues the discussion of the phonemic awareness research and provides additional information for drawing conclusions about this key issue.

⊿┛ Less Than Impressive Effect Sizes

ZIP Codes and Reading Achievement

A confusion between correlation and causation runs through the entire "Phonemic Awareness" and "Phonics" sections of the Report and adds its own impediment for understanding the contribution of PA skills in beginning reading. Although the difference between these two concepts should be obvious to anyone claiming to have sufficient scientific expertise to review a body of empirical research and make recommendations for national policy, the simple distinction between causation and correlation appears to have been lost in the NRP Report.

> A confusion between correlation and causation runs through the Report.

ZIP codes, for example, are good predictors of academic achievement.[1] A student's ZIP code (an indication of family income and education, quality of schools in the area, a child's access to educational experiences, etc.) is strongly correlated with future school success. However, this correlation does not make ZIP codes a cause of academic achievement. Unfortunately, failure to understand the distinction between these two concepts could lead some reading researchers to investigate the possibility that the reading achievement of children in poor, urban areas with terrible schools might improve if they were given the ZIP codes of children in affluent, suburban areas with excellent schools.

Top Predictor

An example of this confusion is the Report's conclusion that one study showed that phonemic awareness was the "top predictor along with letter knowledge" (knowing the names of letters) of later reading achievement. This description suggests that because there was a high correlation between PA and "reading achievement scores" in kindergarten and first grade, PA could "play a causal role in learning to read."[2]

The accuracy of the Report's conclusion becomes questionable, however, when the study's third strongest predictor of reading achievement is also included. That predictor is the degree of success on a "finger localization" test, in which a child whose vision is blocked identifies which of his or her fingers an adult has touched. Despite its predictive correlation with future reading achievement, finger localization skill in itself could not be considered causal to learning to read, and no educator would suggest finger location training as a beginning reading method.

The Report does not mention this predictor and also fails to mention that the researchers, David Share and his colleagues, offered an explicit caveat about confusing correlation with causation. Yes, they did find that letter knowledge was a strong predictor of future reading, but they emphasized its predictive strength did not mean that beginning readers needed to know letter names in order to get off to a fast, secure start in reading. Although "knowledge of letter names has been traditionally considered the single best predictor of reading achievement, there appears to be no evidence that letter-name knowledge facilitates reading acquisition," the researchers observed.[3]

Letter-name knowledge is likely to be part of and represent early experience with and accomplishment in written language activities, and it is knowledge—like that of various skills, such as phonemic awareness—that can be considered to be a marker of these experiences and accomplishments. None of this complexity or these distinctions is captured in the Report's simplistic summary of the "top predictors" of future reading success.

"Effect Size Was Impressive"

A striking example of congruence between the Panel's interpretation of the research and the Panel's assumptions about the best reading instruction is the Report's description of a study by Fiona Brennan and Judith Ireson. The Report concludes that in this study a PA "treatment group" was "compared to one no-treatment group" and the "effect size was impressive." This provides evidence, the Report states, that the training program being studied could be "used effectively in American classrooms."[4]

The Report does not tell readers that there were *two* control groups, not one. In addition to the no-treatment group, another control group learned PA in an "as needed" way, that is, the children were taught specific skills as the teacher identified the children's need for them. In other words, we have here a study that did what the studies reviewed up until now did not do: it compared two different approaches for teaching skills. Hence, we have an opportunity to compare children learning PA skills through a training program, as the studies reviewed up until now have used, with children learning PA through an as-needed approach. Although this comparison would have allowed the Panel to delve into the question of how these skills should be taught and learned, it did not do so. Therefore, we will.

> *Superior scores on phonemic awareness tasks did not correspond to higher scores on reading tasks.*

At the end of the school year, the researchers found that the training group did significantly better on phonemic awareness tests. However, they also found "no significant differences between the [skills training and as-needed teaching] groups on the tests that matter the most, those of word reading and spelling." This finding the Report does not mention. The researchers observed that "the significantly superior scores achieved by the training group in this study on tasks of phonemic awareness suggest that this group should also achieve higher scores on the reading tasks, but this was not in fact the case." These conclusions too are not quoted in the Report.

> *Skills can be learned within holistic reading activities.*

The researchers went on to propose that the "writing experiences" of the as-needed group might have accounted for their reading success. On average, they "wrote longer stories than either" the training group or the "normal" kindergarten group.[5] These conclusions too are omitted from the Report.

The study showed, in other words, that children can learn rhyme, syllable synthesis, word reading, and spelling without a skills-training program. Moreover, extensive writing activities are likely to be effective for attaining the literacy knowledge for which the researchers tested. This study also lends some support to a holistic written language approach insofar as it indicates that PA skills can be readily learned within a rich array of reading and writing activities. And it further demonstrates that there not only is no need for a stepwise approach to literacy learning but that such an approach can reduce time spent on essential and productive literacy activities, such as writing experiences.

"The Training Benefited Children's Decoding Skill"

Another study that receives special attention in the Report compared Australian kindergartners in a phonemic skills training program with another group of kindergartners and, the Report states, found that "at the end of each successive grade," the skills-training "group read significantly more pseudowords than controls, indicating that the training benefited children's decoding skill."[6]

Technically, this description is correct: the training group did do better than a control group that spent its time classifying items by color, shape, edibility, and other characteristics. The absurdity of this comparison and, therefore, the utter scientific uselessness of this study are obvious, given the absence of any reading activity for the control group, who indeed might as well have been making muffins. The absurdity, however, does not end here. What the Report does not say is that the pseudoword test was only one among several. There were also tests of spelling regular words, irregular words, and pseudowords. There were tests of reading regular and irregular words. And, yes, there was a test of reading pseudowords. Of the entire six tests, five showed no significant group differences at the end of first grade, pointing to a decided absence of a skills-training effect not noted in the Report. The Report also fails to say that at the end of second grade, even though there was still a significant difference in reading pseudowords, the difference was less than extraordinary: on a list of 20 pseudowords, the training group read an average of 17.03 correctly, and the controls read 15.57 correctly.

The Report continues: "At the end of 2nd grade, there was a marginal difference in reading comprehension favoring the PA trained students."[7] Use of the term *marginal* (that is, not statistically significant) suggests a curious willingness to soften scientific standards in order to make the best case for skills training. An even greater softening—in fact, a complete abandonment—of scientific standards is apparent when we see how the test for reading comprehension was devised and conducted. The Report does not tell readers that the researchers themselves created the reading comprehension test and administered it orally. The researchers did not explain why they did not use a more objective measure, such as a standardized achievement test administered by school personnel not associated with the study. Finally, and perhaps most damaging to the results of the study, was a potential conflict of interest: the researchers, Brian Byrne and Ruth Fielding-Barnsley, were "testing" a training program (Sound Foundations) that they themselves had created and wished the Australian schools would use.[8] This detail is also omitted from the Report.

"A Similar Study"

Nowhere is the extent of the Report's predilection to make facts fit conclusions more vividly displayed than in its rendering of two 1993 articles on Reading Recovery, an early intervention program. The Report states that the authors of one article, Sandra Iversen and William Tunmer,[9] "conducted a similar study" to one reported by William Tunmer and Wesley Hoover[10] and that both studies showed that, by receiving "systematic phonics instruction" in a modified Reading Recovery program, students were able to complete the program in "less time" than it took the students in the regular Reading Recovery program. This, the Report argues, makes "the more intensive phonics approach preferable."[11]

From this description, readers of the Report would conclude that the power of systematic phonics instruction was replicated in two studies. In fact, the two publications are not about two studies but are only two articles about the same study. Anyone examining the two articles will wonder how this misrepresentation could have been made, because the authors themselves discuss only one study, and the articles contain charts of the identical means and standard deviations for scores on letter identification, word recognition, writing vocabulary, and several other tests.

Anyone dealing with a large number of empirical studies is likely to make some mistakes in details, anything from an incorrect first or last name to mistyped or misquoted figures. I have made these errors myself and can readily excuse them in any work surveying numerous quantitative studies. But I submit that the misrepresentation of one study as two, especially when considered within the array of the Report's misrepresentations, suggests a breach of scholarly thoroughness that was committed in the throes of mustering "evidence" in a rush to judgment.

In addition to the misrepresentations, let us look more closely at the Report's conclusion that the students trained in intensive phonics completed the program in less time. As I said, two forms of Reading Recovery were compared. In the standard approach, once children could identify at least thirty-five of the fifty-two upper- and lowercase letters of the alphabet, the portion of time devoted to learning letters was replaced by additional storybook reading, in which word analysis activities such as phonemic awareness were learned as needed within the reading activity. Within the modified program, this time was devoted to the direct teaching of phonemic skills. Both interventions produced similar phonemic awareness and reading test scores at the end of the school year, showing that skills can be learned through direct teaching as well as within more holistic reading activities.

But the Report does not leave it there. Although the test results were similar, because the modified Reading Recovery group ended its work in eight and a half weeks and the standard group in eleven and a half weeks, it demonstrated that the "more intensive phonics approach" was "preferable," according to the Report. Although this three-week difference might be significant for some school budgets, I suggest that, within an entire school year, it would be minor, especially because of the comparable literacy achievement at year's end. Furthermore, a shorter completion time of an intervention program is not necessarily either more efficient or preferable. There could be benefits within the time differences that do not fit into the meta-analysis or the Report's conception of reading education. For example, a longer intervention program and greater emphasis on reading storybooks could contribute to reading pleasure and motivation, to thinking more deeply about stories, and to gaining confidence in discussing stories, all of which could have lasting influences on reading development. Given the boundaries of the meta-analysis and the Report's narrow range of vision, possibilities such as these appear to be beyond the pale; at the very point when a study might encourage additional thinking, the meta-analysis—that is, the Report—stops its observations.

Sidestepping the "Simple Theory"

The NRP describes another study as one that added PA training to a Reading Recovery program and showed that "effect sizes, though small, favored the PA-training group" for reading and spelling.[12] The problem with this summary is that it is false: there was no Reading Recovery program!

The researchers compared three combinations of phonemic training and reading instruction. One group received "PA training alone" (tasks such as blending and segmenting phonemes and rhyming words). A second group, called the "reading with phonology" group, used a modified Reading Recovery model that added the PA training program to the standard Reading Recovery activities of reading and rereading books, writing stories, and relating PA activities to the stories. At the completion of the study, the "phonology training alone" group had finished the entire PA training program, whereas "the reading with phonology" group finished approximately half of it.

A third group, a "reading alone" group, used a contorted model of Reading Recovery. That is, the students did writing and reading activities similar to those of the second group, but, unlike the Reading Recovery method—or virtually anything resembling good instruction!—the teacher omitted any explicit reference to letter-sound relationships and sequences. Regardless of how much a teacher recognized a child's need to learn a skill, regardless of how much a child might express a desire to learn a skill, the experiment allowed none to be taught.

Approximately a year after the various forms of instruction were completed, the groups were compared, and the "reading with phonology" group (which completed only *half* the PA training activities), not the PA training group, was found to have statistically superior test results in reading comprehension, word identification, and spelling. This finding is connected to a basic aim in the study's design, one fully omitted in the Report: the researchers undertook to examine what they described as the prevailing "simple theory that there is a direct causal path from phonological skills to reading skills." For example, Marilyn Adams, Barbara Foorman, and their colleagues, in the introduction to their phonemic awareness training program manual, state, "a child's level of phonemic awareness on entering school is widely held to be the strongest single determinant of the success that she or he will experience in learning to read—or, conversely, the likelihood that she or he will fail."[13]

> The researchers concluded that PA "training alone is not a powerful way [to improve] children's reading skills."

Upon completion of their experiment, however, contrary to the "simple theory," Hatcher and his colleagues concluded that PA "training alone is not a powerful way of improving children's reading skills." Although the "phonology training alone" group "made significantly more progress" in learning phonemic skills than did the other groups, this superiority did not translate into comparably superior literacy test scores. Consequently, they proposed that their findings "cast doubt on the simple theory that there is a direct causal path from phonological skills to reading skills."[14] None of these conclusions is quoted in the Report.

Does the study show that effect sizes "favored the PA-trained group," as the Report explains?[15] No. Not only does the Report omit the researchers' own conclusions about the causal role of phonemic awareness in learning to read, but it also fails to discuss the bizarre "reading alone" group, with its potentially damaging teaching method, which I hope cannot be found in any actual classroom. The group is hardly a foil demonstrating the superior effect sizes of the "PA-trained" group.

A "Greater Number" of Comprehension Studies

As I have discussed, the essential test of the Report's claims about the effects of PA training must be outcomes in long-term reading comprehension and achievement. It is this outcome that one researcher in the last chapter referred to as the "strong test of intervention" and another researcher concluded was an "assumption" of the research on PA training but one that still lacked "direct evidence." Advocates of PA training might state that the connection is there but indirectly; that is, PA training leads to mastery of other skills, which in turn promotes fluency and other skills, which in their turn have a close causal influence on comprehension. However, without direct evidence of the effectiveness of this sequence, it remains a conjecture unworthy of guiding national policy on reading instruction.

In a later paper, in the journal *Reading Research Quarterly*, Linnea Ehri and other panelists presented a reprise of the Report's section on phonemic awareness and gave special attention to studies that supposedly demonstrated that PA instruction "did improve students' reading comprehension."[16]

Ehri and her colleagues identified ten studies, from which twenty statistical relationships were derived, for evaluating the effects of phonemic skills training on reading comprehension. Among the twenty, six supposedly showed a large effect, six showed a moderate effect, and eight showed either a small or a negative effect.[17] We will look most closely at the strongest evidence presented.

Three "Large" Effects

Three of six "large" effects came from a single study,[18] not three different studies, a revealing fact not mentioned in the Report and obtainable only through extensive exploration of numerous details in an appendix in the Report.[19]

This study divided poor readers into four groups, two of which received training in sound categorization (for example, learning which words share beginning, middle, and ending sounds). In addition to this training, one of these two groups used plastic letters in helping them learn the shared sounds. The third group learned how to classify word and picture cards into categories (for example, *hen* and *bat* are animals). All three of these groups had the training added to their regular classroom instruction. The fourth group had classroom instruction only. At the end of the two-year training period, the two groups that received training in sound categorization had scores in reading and spelling that were statistically superior to those of the other groups, with the group that had also used plastic letters scoring better than the one that had not.

> *The large effects on comprehension were derived from comparisons of PA training versus no instructional alternative.*

Thus the large effects on reading comprehension that the Report alludes to were derived from comparisons of PA training versus either no training or categorizing words and pictures. Once again, we see how the experimental model referred to in the "compared with what?" question encourages unequal results. The study showed that specific training in phonemic awareness, with and without learning letter-sound relationships, can help children earn better reading comprehension and spelling scores than if they were not to receive any alternative instructional approach that included phonemic awareness, but that is all it showed.

With respect to the charge from Congress, we may ask, What "various approaches" are included in this study that would help in evaluating the merits of various approaches if no group was engaged in a meaningful instructional alternative? Moreover, because the two publications about this study offer no information about regular classroom reading instruction, we can draw no conclusions about the classroom instruction that this training supported and needs to support for promoting reading comprehension.

The Effect of "Cutting, Coloring, and Sticking"

The fourth large effect on reading comprehension was found in a study conducted in Spain. After pitting a variety of skills-training groups against a group that spent its session time "coloring, cutting, and sticking, etc.," researchers Sylvia Defior and Pio Tudela found that the skills-training group that used sounds and letters to make words benefited most in later reading test scores.[20]

And the regular classroom curriculum? The original paper says only that reading instruction "began with a global approach, using familiar and simple utterances and followed by a more analytical phase, where they focused on phonemes."[21] Little additional information is provided. Perhaps the "global method" refers to sight-word instruction. I suggest this because the researchers refer to work such as Jeanne Chall's that, the researchers explain, has "generally favored the phonetic over the global methods."[22] If this, indeed, is the source of the term, it refers to "look-say" (sight-word) instruction. This would mean that the study had a straw man contrast and offers no contribution for guiding reading instruction, because no one is currently advocating "look-say" beginning reading instruction. Beyond this kind of oblique explanation of classroom instruction, we simply have no information to determine the kind of reading and writing taught, the way in which phonemes became the "focus," and so on. Hence, we are left with another example of scientific rigor: PA training has a bigger effect on comprehension than does "cutting, coloring, and sticking" and enhances regular classroom instruction about which we know next to nothing!

Instruction Starts at Seven and a "Parts-to-Whole" Approach

The last two studies that were supposed to demonstrate a large effect on comprehension can be briefly summarized. One was done in Finland, where "formal reading and spelling instruction starts the year the child reaches seven years of age," and contained the familiar "compared with what?" problem. While one group of kindergartners was in a PA training program for the entire kindergarten year, thereby receiving a total of two years of written language instruction by the end of first grade, the children in the control group received no alternative written language instruction in kindergarten and, therefore, had only one year of instruction at the end of first grade.[23]

The final study showing a large effect is even less useful for any kind of effect size analysis because the regular first-grade classroom instruction used a "basal reading series," which the researcher, Sue Weiner, described as a "phonics program" that went from "part-to-whole," a fact the Report fails to mention.[24] Consequently, we have a study in which PA training is appended to phonics classroom instruction, leading to the insight that children taught with a beginning reading "parts-to-whole" reading program could use the addition of more parts training. It is reasonable to conclude that this study offers nothing for informing national reading legislation.

No "Unique Benefits"

These were the studies that supposedly demonstrated large effects on comprehension. Another study, unlike most of the PA training studies reviewed in the Report, actually did follow-up testing one and two years after training, at which time there were no group differences found on either of two reading comprehension tests. The researchers recognized that, "as in other studies, this amount of [phonemic awareness] training did not lead to unique benefits for growth in reading comprehension or in later differences in word reading over similar amounts of reading training with less explicit training in phonological skills." This outcome, they observed, was "similar to the findings of most controlled studies of explicit training even with somewhat longer training times."[25]

Reading = "Say *Vef* Without the /V/ Sound"

If the question of how much word reading should count as reading is a significant one, consider how much a study that used only the reading of nonsense words as an outcome measure should be included in the pool of studies on the effects of PA on reading. Such a study, coauthored by panelist Linnea Ehri, taught one group of kindergartners to segment five lists of thirty nonword blends using letter tokens (for example, What are the separate sounds in *ef*?). Another group segmented the blends by just hearing the sounds, not using the letter tokens. The control group received no training of any kind. The training lasted several days, depending on how long it took a child to learn the five lists of words.[26]

The Report described a very short-term study, using no actual words, as showing a significant effect of PA on reading.

At end of the training period, the training group that used the letter tokens did best on tests segmenting nonsense words into phonemes, deleting phonemes in nonsense words ("Say *vef* but without the /v/ sound"), decoding nonsense words, and similar segmentation tasks. Certainly the public should know that research that this national panel on reading education thought might offer direction for national policy—research that the Report described as demonstrating a moderately high effect size on reading—was this very short-term study that used no actual words, provided no experience in actual beginning reading, and had no control group engaged in another written language approach.

Boosting the Distar Phonics Program

Of all the studies in the Report's "Phonemic Awareness" section, this is one of the most irrelevant for deciding anything about reading instruction policy.

This five-week study by Rollanda O'Connor and Joseph Jenkins used ten kindergartners classified as developmentally delayed and instructed them in Reading Mastery (formerly Distar), a purely phonics program that provides "direct instruction in letter-sound correspondence" through the practice of saying and blending sounds and "reading and rereading sentences and passages composed of highly controlled, decodable text" (text containing many phonetically consistent words).[27] These children also received twenty sessions of individual spelling instruction and afterward were compared with ten similar children who were taught with Reading Mastery only. Post-tests showed that the Reading Mastery plus spelling group had superior scores on spelling and word reading measures.

What are we to make of these findings other than the following: a purely phonemic awareness and phonics program was found to be insufficient for developmentally delayed children if spelling instruction was not added? Or, that learning to spell helps learning to read? As vacuous as these results are, except for those interested in knowing about the merits of the Reading Mastery program, the study met the Report's scientific standards and its effect size results contributed to the Report's recommendations.

A "Causal Link"

Also irrelevant for national reading policy is a study that began with one four-day experiment with preschool and kindergarten prereaders. These preschoolers were divided into one group that was trained to segment four spoken syllables into their initial consonant and remaining portion of the word (e.g., hem is made of /h/ and /em/) and a control group that was trained simply to repeat the syllables aloud. Both groups were then taught to do a reading task on learning words related or unrelated to the spoken syllables they had learned. The trained group made fewer mistakes in learning words related to the sound patterns they had practiced in training. A second four-day experiment used another form of phonemic training, and again the trained children made fewer mistakes learning words related to the sounds in which they had been trained. From these brief studies, researchers Rebecca Treiman and Jonathan Baron drew the slightly hyperbolic conclusion that "these results suggested a causal link between" phonemic awareness abilities "and the ability to benefit from spelling-sound relations in reading."[28] The hyperbole was carried into the Report, which calculates the effect on reading found in this diminutive study to be between moderate and large.

"Superior" Reading Performance

Perhaps the following study is even more inconsequential than the previous two.

Done in the mid-1970s, this study, conducted in a single session, taught one group of four- to six-year-old children to read and blend sounds in words containing consonant-vowel-consonant combinations (e.g., *pip*, *tin*, *not*) and another group just to read the words. At the end of the session, on a test of reading simple words, the researchers found that the performance of the blending and reading group was "superior" to the performance of the group that just read words. This finding from a single session was translated into the Report as demonstrating a large effect in reading.[29]

How Is Phonemic Awareness Acquired?

Absent in the Report is any substantial reasoning about how phonemic awareness is learned. For example, the Report acknowledges that when children enter school, they will have differing degrees of phonemic awareness and "some will need more instruction than others."[30] One of the key questions the Report does not ask is, How does it happen that many children acquire phonemic awareness prior to entering school without ever having had specific, explicit training in it? By not posing the question, the Panel is able to ignore the body of research that demonstrates that PA develops in the preschool years through immersion in a rich written language environment (storybook reading, rudimentary writing, word-sound songs, etc.). Within the written language activities, experiences, and interactions, children also develop knowledge of letter names, vocabulary, syntax, simple words, and numerous other facets of written language. Again, the growth of literacy competence through immersion in these rich written language environments is not due to any training in essential skills. Phonemic awareness, therefore, although

> PA is a marker of access to literacy opportunities and experiences, not an isolated skill to be trained.

an important part of early literacy development, needs to be seen as a marker of access to extensive literacy opportunities and experiences, not an isolated skill that needs to be trained.

One marker of the Report's failure to consider this perspective is evident in its statement that socioeconomic status (SES) "exerted no impact on effect size, indicating that low and mid-to-high SES children benefited similarly from PA training in acquiring phonemic awareness."[31] The Report addresses SES from one direction only and thereby omits important findings about the relationship between social class and reading skills that could lead to very different conclusions from those in the Report.

Research does show that social class experiences have a major impact on the development of children's written language abilities, including phonemic awareness. Furthermore, research shows that because they are more likely to have a rich written language environment, most children from middle-income families acquire greater knowledge in phonemic awareness and other language knowledge than do children from lower-income families.

For example, a study by psychologist Christopher Lonigan and his colleagues shows that on a variety of phonemic awareness tasks, preschoolers from middle-income families did dramatically better than did children from low-income families. The respective test scores for blending words were 93.8 versus 26.7; for blending syllables, 89.2 versus 13.3; and for blending phonemes, 80.0 versus 6.7. All but one of the middle-income children knew at least some letter names, compared with 62 percent of lower-income children. Thirty-eight percent of the middle-income preschoolers could read at least one word, but the lower-income children could read *none*.[32]

The superior scores are outcomes of supports, activities, materials, experiences, and general contexts in which the term *phonemic awareness* was not likely to be known nor the skill directly taught. They are outcomes of more daily reading, more play with literacy materials, more time in better preschools, and more access to educational and educating resources. The recognition of the implications of these early social-class-related differences in PA competence outcomes means very different conclusions about educational and social policy that will promote phonemic awareness. Seeing PA as the Report does leads to the highly inadequate question: What kind of training programs are required to teach phonemic awareness? Seeing phonemic awareness as a marker, however, leads to the richer, more promising question: How can all young children obtain the comprehensive written language experiences and materials, the array of educational supports, services, and enrichment that have been shown to produce literacy achievement?" This view of reading acquisition is dramatically different from that found both in the Report and in the Bush reading legislation.

Conclusion

The contentious issue is not whether PA is an important part of learning to read. It is obvious that it is and as I have written elsewhere, recognition of its contribution runs through the literature on emergent (early) literacy, writing, and literature-based teaching.[33] Those who hold high the PA skills-training banner did not exactly discover the benefit of PA in beginning reading. Twenty years ago, emergent literacy researchers Emilia Ferreiro and Ana Teberosky, for example,

> The Report has few studies that evaluated alternative instructional approaches to teaching skills.

were reporting research on how young children acquired PA in their experience and experiments in writing.[34] What is at issue and has always been at issue is how PA is learned and how it should be taught.

What has this Report proven about PA? Beyond the Report's meta-analysis and summaries of the studies, the methodological problems in the research and the Report's misrepresentations in its evidence and conclusions are extensive and glaring. Most studies had narrow measures of reading. Most of the control groups either learned no skills or were taught with dubious, straw man beginning reading approaches that few current reading educators advocate. A large number of studies were minuscule and short-term, and the few that did have long-term follow-up failed to show long-term benefits on comprehension. Remarkably absent are genuine alternative approaches to teaching skills that would provide a true contrast in findings. In the few instances where they are included, the studies show that teaching skills in an as-needed model for promoting reading achievement is at least as effective as PA training. There was little research on the value of writing in learning skills, and where such evidence existed, the Report gave it little emphasis. Repeatedly, the Report slants its interpretations to fit prior conclusions about what counts in beginning reading instruction. The Report frequently ends thinking about complex issues concerning PA at the very point that it should encourage it. An accurate evaluation of the studies used in the Report actually undercuts any claims about the substantial benefits of phonemic awareness training on reading.

Systematic Phonics Beats Whole Language!

The second half of the Report's "Alphabetics" section is a review of phonics studies, thirty-eight in all. In our examination of the phonemic awareness research, we saw that there were very few studies that actually compared alternative instructional approaches. The phonics studies contain a few more such comparisons, some of which look at phonics versus whole language teaching. Summarizing the conclusions of the effect size analysis, the Report states that "students taught systematic phonics outperformed students who were taught a variety of nonsystematic or non-phonics programs including basal programs, whole language approaches, and whole word programs." Because of the importance of legitimate instructional comparisons, this chapter will examine the studies that used a whole language or "meaning" approach and assess whether systematic phonics, as the Report claims, did "produce better reading growth."[1]

"Few Overall Differences"

The first study we will review compared whole language and "phonics/skills-based" second-grade classroom instruction. In the former,

> *The data contradict the Report's conclusion about the "better reading growth" in skills-emphasis classrooms.*

skills were taught as needed, using the contexts of story reading and writing to teach the skill, but when poor readers needed particular skills, the teacher did teach them in isolation. In the phonics/ skills classrooms, skills were taught through direct instruction, independently of story reading.

At the end of second grade, the children in both classrooms had comparable scores on tests of word recognition in isolation and in context and comparable scores in passage comprehension. There were "few overall differences" between the two teaching groups, researchers Kay Wilson and Charles Norman concluded.[2] The students did differ on one word identification test (a cloze test, in which a student identifies deleted words in sentences), and this one favored the whole language group! Surprisingly, although the phonics/skills approach emphasized letter-sound information, students taught with this approach did not use this information "significantly more for word identification than students taught in a whole language approach."[3] These results are especially revealing because a chief argument for explicit phonics programs is that they give beginning readers a boost in word identification, an argument not supported here. The data from this study, then, contradict the Report's conclusions about the "better reading growth" in skills-emphasis over whole language classrooms.

Learning the "Alphabetic Principle"

The next study too compared the effectiveness of direct instruction of phonics skills in traditional classrooms and a whole language approach that emphasized meaning and comprehension and taught phonics less explicitly, relying more on the process of self-discovery of alphabetic principles through writing and reading.

> *Children in whole language classes learned the "alphabetic principle through extensive writing and exposure to print."*

At the end of the school year, these first graders, many of whom were from low-income families, showed no significant group differences in measures of reading comprehension, vocabulary, phonemic awareness, decoding, spelling, and writing. Contrary to what one would surmise from just reading the Report, the study also confirmed that "children in a whole language program" can "learn the alphabetic principle through extensive writing and extensive exposure to print."

Beyond the similar test outcomes and their implications for choosing among instructional approaches, the researchers were disappointed to find that neither instructional approach was sufficient for closing the gap between the students with low and high incoming reading skills. This outcome raises an important issue that has been minimized in the debate over beginning literacy instruction and totally ignored in the Report: focusing on instruction exclusively and neglecting a more comprehensive policy toward the hardships faced by poor children is likely to produce disappointing results regardless of the educational approach employed. Reading experts—and especially those on the NRP—tend to focus on components of beginning reading and to neglect the numerous other aspects of children's lives that influence their learning. I will say more about this in the chapters ahead.

For now, focusing primarily on the Report's claims, the conclusions of researchers Janell Klesius and colleagues are instructive. They concluded that the comparable results indicated that skills-emphasis, scripted programs were not necessary: "with little inservice, teachers could make a transition to whole language without loss in student achievement. It appears to be possible for teachers to abandon teachers' manuals which include a detailed scope and sequence of skills as well as detailed lesson plans."[4] This judgment is not quoted in the Report.

Let us turn to another study for evidence the Report claims in support of its conclusions.

"At a Level Equal To"

First graders in a class using a skills-emphasis basal reading program that included little writing were compared with other students in a whole language class that taught phonics "indirectly through the examination of words with similar spelling (e.g., words beginning with the same consonant or ending with the same phonogram)" and in "daily writing activities."[5] Like the previous studies I have discussed, at the end of the school year, this study found no group differences in tests of word recognition, reading comprehension, or spelling phonetically predictable words and nonsense words.

And, as in the previous studies, the groups had similar success in learning skills: even though "children in the whole language instruction classroom did not receive direct phonics instruction, overall they appeared able to use letter-sound correspondence information to decode words at a level equal to that of the children who had received direct instruction in phonics sounds." Moreover, "the children in the whole language classroom could read nonsense words at a level equal to that of children" in the skills-emphasis classroom.[6] Researchers Priscilla Griffith and her colleagues regarded this as especially telling because the nonsense words test was aimed solely at testing phonics skills. None of these observations is in the Report.

Nothing about writing in whole language classes is mentioned in the Report.

Beyond the similarities, the researchers noted one important difference: The children in the whole language classroom "engaged daily in multiple writing experiences" and consequently "wrote more words and used more unique words in their compositions than did the children in the traditional classroom." Furthermore, the children in the whole language classrooms wrote more fluently. The trade-off appears to have been that they were "less concerned about spelling words correctly."[7] However, test results showed that at that point in their literacy development, their spelling was not worse than that of children in skills-emphasis classrooms. Nothing about writing in whole language classes is mentioned in the NRP Report.

Unfortunately, these comparable outcomes still meant that both kinds of classes continued to have underachieving readers, again indicating that instructional policy needs to be part of a larger policy approach. Although the researchers did not provide any information about the children's backgrounds beyond saying that they lived in "a rural school district," we may assume that, as is common in rural areas, at least some of the children were poor, had limited preschool education, had less access to print, and had life stressors that might have impeded learning.

"Try Different Keywords"

In *Misreading Reading*, I devoted an entire chapter to this next study, by Barbara Foorman and her colleagues,[8] and therefore will now only highlight a few key conclusions.[9] Praised in the media and by proponents of skills-emphasis teaching as the premier study demonstrating the superiority of direct instruction over whole language, the "Foorman study," as it was commonly called, received extensive publicity and acclaim, much of it based on what Foorman and her coauthors, for over a year prior to its actual publication, insisted were their research findings.

Direct instruction emphasizing skills did not produce superior reading comprehension.

Following the study's publication, and because of continued controversy over its results, I obtained the original data—thanks largely to the Freedom of Information Act—and conducted an in-depth analysis of the results of the two approaches: "direct code" (as the direct, skills-emphasis instruction of the Open Court reading program was called) versus "embedded code" (as the "whole language" control group was called). Looking at the test results for the first- and second-grade classrooms in the schools used in the study, I concluded that overall, both teaching approaches produced about the same achievement outcomes in reading comprehension, but neither approach had a satisfactory impact for students; that is, poor readers remained poor readers. This conclusion did not address the question of whether the classes the researchers identified as whole language actually met that description. Regardless, it is clear that direct instruction emphasizing skills did not produce superior reading comprehension. I also did a reanalysis of the results of measures of letter identification, word identification, and reading pseudowords (*dif, giz, blif,* etc.) and found that, as was true for reading comprehension results, overall test performances for both groups were comparable. Foorman and her colleagues later claimed that I manipulated data in my reanalysis, but when I requested evidence for the charge, they were not able to provide it (see Appendix).

A word about the Open Court reading program. To date, school systems across the nation are purchasing it; it is now, for example, only one of two reading programs that California school systems are allowed to buy with state education funds. These purchases are based primarily on the assumption that, unlike whole language, it is a research-based program. What the school systems appear not to know is that this 1998 Foorman paper remains the single published research paper attempting to demonstrate its effectiveness. When I began research for *Misreading Reading,* McGraw-Hill, the publisher of the Open Court program, repeatedly cited the Foorman study as its "research-based" evidence. Now, perhaps because of the criticism of the study, in the "Research" section of the Open Court website, the Foorman publication is noticeably absent.[10] Currently, one finds only results reported from school districts in California, "research" authored by a McGraw-Hill employee that has yet to appear in an educational journal. To be certain the Foorman study was not somewhere else on the website, I tried to find "Foorman" with the website search engine but received the following response: "There are no matches for your search query. Please try different keywords."

Ignoring Other "Variables Influencing Students' Growth"

Concerned that "the current movement toward whole language is also a movement away from phonics," Lloyd Eldridge modified a whole language program by including a daily fifteen-minute period of total-class systematic, intensive, and direct phonics instruction and compared the outcomes of this approach with one using a basal reading program that also included the direct teaching of phonics.[11] The students in the study were first graders from low socioeconomic families, with the largest student turnover in the school district. The researcher emphasized that although the "modified whole language approach used in this study differed markedly from generally accepted whole language approaches," the whole language classrooms spent the majority of time on activities common in whole language teaching.[12]

The teachers using the basal reading program also read to children daily, but not until later in the school year, rather than right from the start, as the whole language program did. Unlike whole language teaching, the basal instruction tended not to integrate all of the language arts, even though the children did write stories and other texts each day. Basal instruction, in contrast to whole language teaching, limited social interaction and student collaboration.

At the end of the school year, the students in the modified whole language program "made greater vocabulary gains, comprehension gains, and total reading gains than students involved in the basal program."[13] There were also significant differences in the children's attitudes toward reading, with the whole language students having a more positive one. Recall from Chapter 2 that attitude was a key concern of reading teachers surveyed. For the Report, however, it was not a topic deserving examination.

Because the modified whole language approach used a variety of practices and the study did not include a whole language classroom that taught phonics skills "as needed," it is hard to identify the phonics program as the key difference affecting the outcome measures. What is clear, however, from the researcher's description of whole language practices, is that this teaching provided a richer literacy education than was provided in the basal reader classroom. These practices included the following:

- Integrating the language arts—reading, writing, and spelling—into comprehensive literacy learning activities and themes, rather than treating them as separate subjects. Also integrating other aspects of learning, such as music, social studies, and science, into these activities and themes.
- Organizing literacy learning around themes and units of study that emerged from children's backgrounds, interests, and ideas.
- Encouraging children to write as soon as they enter school because writing helps children learn many facets of written language, including sound-symbol relationships. Using children's vocabulary and syntax in numerous written language activities, such as writing messages, letters, and stories, in the process of learning to read, write, and spell.
- Using stories that contained natural language and predictable language patterns.
- Stressing social relationships and interactions among students as they engaged in literacy learning.
- Encouraging children to share readings and writings, to listen and speak with one another about stories they had written and stories they had read, and to share books. Encouraging children to teach and learn from one another and to work collaboratively.

> *The reading outcomes of whole language teaching were superior to those of basal instruction.*

The Report calculated that the modified whole language teaching produced a large statistical effect in comprehension and attributed this to the addition of the phonics program. Because there was no unmodified whole language control, as I said, this interpretation of the effect has no empirical support one way or another. The researcher himself noted that a "major weakness of this study," as in other studies of this kind, was that the "variables influencing students' growth" were "difficult to define, identify, and control."[14]

What is clear from this study is that both approaches taught phonics directly and that the reading outcomes of whole language teaching were superior to those of basal instruction. We can only wonder why the Report considered the array of whole language classroom practices enumerated by the researcher to be inconsequential to the reading outcomes.

This Is Not Whole Language

A study by Mary Ann Evans and Thomas Carr is listed in the Report as one that included whole language teaching, when in fact it did not! Rather, the researchers called it "language-experience" instruction (instruction based primarily on stories derived from children's experiences and dictated by them), although it was not exactly that either. The children in these classes first dictated stories to a teacher, then constructed their own bank of sight words drawn from the stories, and they needed to master 150 sight words "before [they were] to be involved in any group instruction *using basal or published materials*."[15] There is no information about what the teachers in the classrooms did with these basals or other materials. This instruction was compared with a basal reading program that included skills workbooks and phonics drills, and year-end testing found that the children in the total-basal classrooms did better on various reading tests. Given the paucity of information about actual teaching in the "language-experience" group and the apparent inclusion of basal reading programs in it, one cannot say exactly what was proven in this experiment. Whatever it might have been, it was not about whole language.

Neither Is This Whole Language

Although this next study is also described in the Report as one evaluating whole language teaching, it too was not. Working with "at-risk" children, researchers Carol Santa and Torleiv Hoien taught one group with an individual tutoring program that included book reading, word study, writing, and "systematic, explicit instruction" in phonemic analysis.[16] Other "at-risk" children, taught in "small groups," not individually, also read books but did no writing. When a child encountered a word he or she did not know, the tutor "reminded" the child to use clues such as initial letter, vowel pattern, or context. No other skills teaching was described. It is this control group that the Report labels whole language.[17]

Outcome measures showed better results for children in the first group. Once again, we encounter the now-familiar "compared with what?" problem: individual tutoring was found to be superior to group tutoring; teaching word skills was found to be more effective than not teaching them; writing was found to be more effective than no writing.

Beyond this, there were findings of importance in within-group differences that are not mentioned in the Report's rendition of this investigation. When the researchers divided these "at-risk" children into "high-risk" and "low-risk" groups, *no statistically significant differences* were found between the low-risk groups—not in spelling, word recognition, or reading comprehension. Summarizing these results, the researchers stated, "the experimental group statistically significantly outperformed the control group" on all post-intervention tests. "However, the differences between experimental and control students reflect the progress by the high-risk experimental group children on all post-intervention tests."[18]

Why were there no differences between the low-risk at-risk groups? The researchers speculated that the similar outcomes could have been attributed to the extra amount of time they spent actually reading books: "We have long known the importance of the practice effect of reading. Perhaps the extra time each day for reading books on an appropriate level of difficulty may be enough to accelerate the performance of most children less at risk."[19] Hence, the study indicates that even for at-risk students, for those who are low-risk, actual

> *The Report's conclusions are misleading, suggestive of poor, hasty scholarship, or worse.*

reading might be most crucial for their reading development. The Report ignores these more complex issues addressed in this research.

All of this is beside the point, however, for the issue at hand: this was *not* a study of whole language. Labeling it in the Report as such, and reporting that the experimental group demonstrated a large effect in reading comprehension over whole language, is not only misleading but suggestive of poor, hasty scholarship, or worse.

Instruction Helps Construct the "Reading Process"

Let's return to the issue of the Report's varying definition of reading and examine another aspect of the term, one that concerns the direction and outcome of reading instruction. Does the particular way in which reading is defined have an impact, explicitly or implicitly, on actual reading instruction? Does that definition eventually shape students' assumptions and practices when they are learning to read, and does it influence what kind of readers they become? Or, perhaps when a youngster eventually learns to read, the outcome will be the same regardless of the definition embedded in any program of instruction. On the other hand, if embedded definitions are likely to produce varying outcomes, could these outcomes be considered a failure according to one standard and a success according to others? And if this is true, does it make sense to judge one study with the definitions of another, thus falling into the proverbial problem of comparing apples and oranges? A study by Penny Freppon provides insights for beginning to answer these questions.

Freppon compared reading outcomes for first-grade children taught with either skills-based or literature-based/whole language instruction. The Report focused on only a single test, the children's oral reading, and found that the groups had comparable rates of accurate word identification. Therefore, in the "oral reading" column in the Report's appendix that outlines research results, the effect size is listed as zero.[20]

But Freppon's study went beyond this single outcome by looking closely at both the way in which the children processed written language while reading and what conceptions of reading they held. She found that even though the literature-based/whole language instruction did not explicitly teach skills, the children in both forms of instruction "were knowledgeable about the importance of decoding" and "successfully used" it in reading.[21] There was no evidence that whole language instruction diminished children's sense of the value of this aspect of reading. This finding accords with other research that found that as children learn to read, they problem solve and, by doing so, attain increased ability to understand causal and reciprocal relationships. As part of this problem solving, they grasp that a key problem to be solved in learning to read is the mastery

> *A study's definition of reading is likely to produce particular kinds of reading processes.*

of connections between graphemes and phonemes.[22]

The similar group knowledge of decoding did not mean that each group used the strategy the same way: the skills-emphasis group used it as a primary one, while the whole language group used it to a lesser degree because that group employed a greater variety of strategies, such as rereading, using context, and skipping words. An unexpected finding was that even though the whole language children "attempted to sound out words less often," when they did attempt it, they "achieved a higher success rate of correctly sounding out words." Their rate was 53 percent compared with 32 percent for the skills-emphasis children.[23]

These findings suggest that a study's particular definition of reading is likely to produce particular kinds of reading processes. The implicit definition of reading in whole language instruction made decoding *a* key, not *the* key, in orchestrating this reading process. For the skills group, the grapheme-phoneme task loomed larger both as a strategy and as the meaning of reading and was more *the* key than *a* key. In the skills classroom, reading for meaning was included, but it was "incidental" to word skills instruction.[24]

The literature-based instruction evoked different thinking and memory use. Decoding skills were included, but more attention was drawn to meaning, with the teacher encouraging the children to think about what was going on in the story. In interviews with the children, the literature-based group expressed greater "understandings of the use of multiple strategies in reading" and "associated reading with language" (whether something makes sense or sounds like a sentence), whereas the skills-emphasis group "expressed understanding of sounding out as a primary reading strategy" and "associated reading with getting words correct."[25] Almost all of the children in the literature group "said that understanding the story or both understanding and getting words right is more important in

> *The literature-based group described a good reader as one that "reads a lot" and "understands the story."*

reading." In contrast, only half the children in the skills group chose these explanations; nearly all of the remaining half chose "getting words right as most important."[26]

Asked about the "characteristics of good readers," the skills group emphasized "knowing and learning words and sounding out words." In contrast, the literature-based group discussed characteristics such as "reading a lot" and "understanding the story." The skills group included "paying attention to the teacher" and "knowing their place in the book," characteristics that were not mentioned by the literature group.[27] These findings could suggest that skills-emphasis teaching tends to encourage conformity and dependence, whereas literature-emphasis teaching tends to encourage independence and self-confidence.

The Freppon study suggests an extremely important conclusion: instruction itself contributes to the construction of the reading process to a considerable degree, and different instruction produces different reading processes. Furthermore, it suggests that the entire model of reading underpinning the Report is false. That is, there is no preordained reading process, and skills-emphasis teaching cannot be said to work better than other instructional approaches because it is better configured to fundamental cognitive processes. Skills-emphasis teaching configures cognition, and in doing so it helps create cognitive processes specifically adequate for accomplishing tasks and reaching goals in that pedagogy. This is very different from assuming that reading achievement goals are invariable, that preestablished cognitive processes must be evoked, and that the best way to do so is with skills-based instruction. These findings also put in serious doubt the theory that children have a limited working memory requiring a youngster to focus on only one kind of beginning reading strategy.[28] It would appear that children can successfully orchestrate several strategies in working memory while not diminishing their ability to identify words and comprehend stories.

Although there is no evidence in this study that children in the literature group have an advantage in standardized test achievement, there is evidence that they were becoming competent in more reading abilities and were acquiring a deeper meaning and appreciation of reading than were the children in the skills-emphasis classes. Finally, this research has useful implications for the questions about which instructional approach is better. This study suggests that the answer depends on the criteria for "better." By conventional, standardized test measures, both groups were comparable and, depending on the criteria, both work. But what is considered "better" and "what works" for skills-emphasis instruction would be unacceptably limited and insufficient for educators and parents who have a different view of what constitutes good reading.

"Produced Better Reading Growth"?

Two studies remain to be mentioned, both of which can quickly be summarized. One was identified as including whole language instruction. Assuming that it did, the researchers found no differences in reading achievement outcomes at the end of first grade between the "whole language" teaching and a phonics program (Distar).[29] The other study, said to assess whole language teaching, was done with children in Britain who were learning English as a second language, "the vast majority" of whom "were Sylheti speakers, with three Cantonese speakers, and four speakers of other languages." This isolated research contains too many differences in student characteristics to be relevant to the Report's purposes.[30]

With the inclusion of these studies, I have reviewed all that supposedly supported the Report's conclusion that "phonics produced better reading growth" than "whole language approaches" and that "students taught systematic phonics outperformed students who were taught" with "whole language approaches."[31]

6 "These [Phonics] Facts Should Persuade Educators and the Public"

The Report's unsubstantiated claim that systematic phonics instruction made a "more significant contribution to children's growth in reading" than did whole language is but one among several such claims about phonics instruction. The Report also maintains that systematic phonics instruction helped "children at risk of developing future reading problems" by producing "substantial reading growth." And "disabled readers" also benefited from this instruction because it helped remediate their "reading difficulties." Systematic phonics instruction is also said to be better than "no phonics instruction," especially when "no-phonics instruction" is the instruction of choice for "kindergartners and 1st graders." This last claim clasps the "compared with what?" problem as if it were a paradigmatic masterpiece rather than a fatal liability. The Report depicts the overall contributions of systematic phonics training as sizable: "A variety of phonics programs have proven effective with children of different ages, abilities, and SES backgrounds," and "these facts should persuade educators and the public that systematic phonics instruction is a valuable part of a successful classroom reading program." In this chapter, as in the last, we will continue to examine "these facts."[1]

"Two Years" of Phonics

"Dyslexic" students (that is, very poor or "disabled" readers) who were enrolled in a hospital's specialized reading clinic were taught with an intensive phonics program for two years. One group of these students was taught by a teacher and another by videotaped instruction. A control group of comparable students also participated, but their teaching fare was a "modified basal reading program," which was the "reading instruction as normally provided in their schools." The clinic students were taught in groups of ten to twelve. No number was provided for how many students were in the regular classrooms, but, given average classroom size, we can assume it exceeded ten to twelve.[2]

At the end of two years, researchers Thomas Oakland and his colleagues found that the gains in reading comprehension, word recognition, and decoding of the two experimental groups were significantly superior to those of the control group. In other words, basal reading instruction with these latter students was found to be inadequate, a finding that would not surprise many reading educators, especially whole language advocates, for whom inherent problems of ineffective basal reader instruction were a strong, initial impetus for trying to create a more successful alternative.

Findings: A phonics program taught to a small number of students in a clinic is superior to a basal reading program in a classroom.

One could summarize this study as showing that within specialized clinical conditions with a small number of students, a phonics program would be superior to a basal reading program taught in a regular-sized school classroom. However, how these results would ultimately transfer to regular classroom teaching and whether they would produce greater success are unanswered questions. For example, it does not follow from this study's results that the phonics program used in the clinic would offer an adequate alternative to the basal readers if it were used in classrooms with the customary much larger number of students. And, as important, although the clinical phonics program achieved better results, these were only relative to those in regular classrooms using basal readers. Even the researchers cautioned that "although the reading gains made by students" in the phonics programs "were clinically significant," that is, their test performance over two years showed beneficial gains compared with their beginning levels, these gains "were relatively modest," especially given the intensity and duration of the intervention.[3] At the end of an extraordinary *two years* of phonics training in groups even smaller than the thirteen to seventeen number that research has shown to be most effective for beginning readers, and in a specialized reading clinic, the students remained "dyslexic" and far behind their normal-reading peers. As a study informing national policy for helping disabled readers, this is hardly a guiding light.

Not Replicated on Standardized Tests

This study also expected more success than it achieved when it taught a group of disabled readers, between eight and thirteen years of age, with a phonics-emphasis program that excluded "explicit training in reading comprehension." In contrast, a second group engaged in written language instruction that focused on "intensive work on oral language comprehension, reading and reading comprehension, and written composition." The control group did no written language work, spending its time learning "classroom survival skills," social skills, classroom etiquette, life skills, and so on. All instruction was in addition to regular schooling, which was not described, and was done with pairs of children.[4]

The results were not exceptional. For researchers Maureen Lovett and her colleagues, the "treatment-specific effects" on skills they believed they observed in the instructional activities were not demonstrated in the "standardized tests" designed "to measure the same skills."[5] The children in the phonics-emphasis program did do better on word recognition tests, but there were no differences among the groups in reading accuracy, reading rate, or reading comprehension!

"Tempered Encouragement" for Meager Results

Maureen Lovett, the primary author of the previous study, led another study, also with disabled readers. This investigation compared one group trained to use phonics and spelling for word recognition with another group that learned words by a whole word method only. As in the previous study, a third group learned only classroom survival skills. At the end of nine weeks, the phonics group did significantly better on tests of word recognition accuracy and speed, but as in the previous study, "encouragement about these positive results" had to be "tempered" because the phonics group did not transfer what they had learned to other reading tasks.[6]

The Report ignores the study's severe methodological limitations.

What are we to conclude from this finding? That teaching whole words in isolation—an approach long deemed by both skills-emphasis and whole language proponents to be inadequate—is not effective? Should not the severe methodological limitations have been evident, prior to even looking at the results, to a panel accumulating evidence for informing national reading policy?

"Quite Effective"?

Two other studies with disabled readers, also led by Maureen Lovett, used two kinds of word identification programs.[7] Here I will discuss the most recent study because it presents the more advanced research design and findings. One group emphasized phonics; another stressed various word recognition strategies, such as "seeking the part of the word that you know."[8]

Not surprisingly, both groups were found to have superior scores than the controls, who, like those in the other Lovett-led studies, were taught school survival skills and not any "specific literacy training."[9] The Report describes the intervention as "quite effective in helping disabled readers improve their reading skills."[10] The Report does not point out that the aim of the research was not only to determine for poor readers whether one of the training programs was superior to the other but to determine whether the two in combination were superior to each separately. And the superiority of this combination—that is, phonics plus various word recognition strategies—was exactly what was found on several measures of reading.

The very limited word-level scope of these instructional interventions severely limits any application of the findings to any classroom reading instruction. We can conclude that beginning readers would be well served if both phonics and word recognition strategies could be used to help them identify unknown words, but this information would add nothing to what classroom teachers already know. The substantial but unanswerable question in this research is whether the narrow skills intervention programs that were used are better than other written language programs for helping disabled readers. Certainly these word-level experimental "treatment conditions" do not meet the definition of "various approaches" in the congressional mandate.[11]

Finally, the meaning of "quite effective," in the Report's summary, quoted earlier, is severely limited because the study focused on a comparison of one disabled group against another. We have no information about whether the narrow treatment programs were much help in enabling poor readers to become normal readers. One would imagine that had these readers made significant advances in their reading, the researchers would have reported that.

Three Studies Showing "Large Effect Sizes"

"No Significant Differences" in Comprehension

We will now turn to three studies that the Report specifically cites as having "indicated that large effect sizes were produced and maintained in the 2nd and 3rd years of instruction for children who were at-risk for future reading problems and who began receiving systematic phonics instruction in kindergarten or 1st grade."[12]

In this first study, the at-risk children were given individual instruction several times a week during the second semester of kindergarten. One group used a program devoted primarily to building phonemic awareness and phonics skills. A second emphasized learning word skills in context as needed, based on the teacher's judgment. A third group engaged in "activities and skills taught in their regular classroom programs," activities that "varied from phonics-oriented activities" to "sight word drill" to "writing in journals or discussing stories that the teacher read."[13]

Researchers Joseph Torgesen and his colleagues described the regular classroom instruction of all three groups as "primarily literature based and guided by a whole-language philosophy, with phonics being taught on an as-needed basis rather than systematically." The extent to which the instruction was fully "guided by a whole-language philosophy" is open to question, but we will accept the researchers' definition and examine the outcome results of the individual tutoring that was at the core of the study.[14]

Among the groups, instructional differences were vivid. The phonics skills group, for example, spent 74 percent of its time on skills activities, while the as-needed group devoted only 26 percent of its time to this work. Conversely, the phonics skills group spent 20 percent of instruction time reading or writing connected text, compared to 57 percent for the skills-as-needed group.

Reading comprehension tests showed no significant differences among a skills-training group, an as-needed group, and the controls.

At the end of second grade, the skills-training group did significantly better on tests of phonemic awareness, decoding, and word recognition than did the as-needed group. On tests of reading comprehension, however, there were *no* significant differences among the three groups. The Report describes this outcome but its dissatisfaction is obvious in the "explanations" it proposes: "One possible explanation" is that the comprehension test was "standardized and not sufficiently sensitive." Or perhaps there were "compensatory processes" (undefined) that were "sufficiently strong to dilute the contribution that superior word recognition skills make to text reading."[15] The possible explanation not proposed is that, indeed, skills-emphasis training does not benefit comprehension as much as the NRP believes it does.

Torgesen and his colleagues addressed comprehension outcomes more forthrightly by noting that "on the one hand, one could argue that" the skills-training "condition was the most effective because it was the only instructional regimen that produced a reliable effect on word level reading skills."[16] But, "on the other hand," they cautioned, "the ability to construct the meaning of written text is the most important outcome of reading instruction and we found no evidence that children in the three instructional groups were reliably different from one another on this variable. Without evidence for differences in comprehension, it is not possible to assert that any one of the instructional approaches in this study was ultimately more effective than the other." They then pointed out that their results were not singular in this regard. Other studies too have "found significant advantages in word level reading skills for children" given direct skills training, "but the differences in reading comprehension were not significant."[17] None of this perspective is quoted in the Report.

"Large Effect Size"?

This second of the three studies that the Report cites as having produced large effect sizes with at-risk children compared "a structured phonics code-emphasis approach" with other teaching that emphasized "uses of context" and meaning. Instructionally, this meant that each group used a basal reading program that the researchers, Idalyn Brown and Rebecca Felton, described as containing one or the other of the two approaches.[18]

At the end of second grade, the at-risk children in the phonics group had significantly higher achievement scores on tests of decoding and word identification. For reading comprehension, however, not only was there "no large effect size" favoring the code-emphasis group, but between the two groups there was no statistically significant difference at all.

If one looks at the effect size chart in the Report's appendix, these specific outcomes are identified in the effect size numbers.[19] For all but the very industrious scholar, however, the Report's summary statement would lead readers to assume that by third grade, "large effect sizes" included comprehension. Once again we see how the Report's varying definition of reading can lead to unwarranted conclusions about effect size.

Also omitted from the Report is any discussion of the basal program that supposedly contained a "context" or "meaning-emphasis" instructional approach. Nor does the Report give as much as a hint that in their 1988 appraisal of basal readers, whole language supporters Kenneth Goodman, Patrick Shannon, Yvonne Freeman, and Sharon Murphy criticized the very basal program used in this study for having "more concern with controlling the sequence of sounds, words, and skills than in providing authentic language in texts." Rather than being meaning-based, they charged, the lessons are "keyed to practicing skills. The story is a means of focusing on and practicing the skills and learning the words, which are the real object of instruction."[20] Consequently, this Brown and Felton study should be seen as pitting one skills-emphasis program against another, with one emerging superior. Furthermore, the study does not demonstrate a legitimate comparison in which "large effects" in decoding and word identification were found.[21]

"A Need" to Test Comprehension, But . . .

The last of the three studies the Report cites as producing large effect sizes with at-risk children compared two groups of first graders. The experimental group began learning to read with a phonemic awareness program and eventually went on to "explicit, systematic instruction" that emphasized "the alphabetic code." The control used the district's "traditional basal reading program," which was supplemented by a phonics workbook. About 25 percent of this group also used a structured phonics program, Reading Mastery.[22] For both groups, a phonetically based spelling program was part of the curriculum.

> *The Report describes a study that did not use a comprehension test as one that showed that skills instruction had a large effect on reading.*

At the end of second grade, the experimental group did better on word recognition but, inexplicably, even though the researchers recommended the "need" for future investigators to study "the influence" of the teaching in this study on comprehension, *no* comprehension test was used in this study.[23] One would assume, of course, that by the end of second grade, that would be precisely the key measure researchers would want to appraise! What are we to conclude about teaching at-risk students from comparing "explicit instruction in the alphabetic code" against a basal reading program with phonics, and, for many children in this second group, the addition of a separate, extensive phonics program? Especially in light of the absence of a comprehension test, how justified is the Report in citing this as one of the three studies that demonstrated large effect sizes?

"Did Not Profit"

A few other studies with at-risk students are worth looking at in order to appraise fully the Report's conclusion that phonics produced "substantial reading growth" for this group.[24]

Reading outcomes of at-risk first graders given one-to-one tutoring in a yearlong phonics program added to regular classroom instruction were compared with outcomes of other at-risk or "not-at-risk" students in the same classrooms, but not in the training program. At the end of second grade, there was no difference in reading comprehension. There was no difference in phonetic analysis. And no difference in decoding. The one significant difference between the at-risk groups was in a word attack test, and that favored the phonics tutoring group. It is this test, extracted from the entire test findings, that the Report identifies as showing a noticeable effect size.

Absent from the Report is the appraisal by researchers Panayota Mantzicopoulos and her colleagues: because "only one robust finding emerged that persisted through second grade," and "since no benefits were noted" on the comprehension test, "it appears that word attack skills may not be sufficient to affect performance in reading comprehension and overall reading achievement in school." Furthermore, they concluded, "contrary to expectation," seriously at-risk children *"did not profit"* from the phonics intervention. "At the end of second grade, [these] children continued to demonstrate significantly subaverage academic performance" on measures of reading. The "moderately at risk" students made advances in phonetic and spelling skills but "no significant gains were noted" on comprehension tests.[25]

Less Than "Robust Effects"

A study of at-risk children in third through sixth grade provided an interesting comparison of a wider range of instructions than is usually found in this research. "Reciprocal teaching," one of these approaches, emphasized "dialogue between teachers and students" while skills and comprehension were being taught to a student who was reading. Another approach was direct, systematic instruction heavily emphasizing phonics and similar skills. A third was computer-assisted instruction. A fourth kind of teaching used a basal reading series. "Effective teaching practices" was the fifth kind; however, the teaching materials used in these practices were not described. Sixth and last was peer tutoring. At the end of ten weeks of instruction, the greatest gains in reading scores (reading aloud, reading silently) were produced in basal reading instruction, reciprocal teaching, and computer-assisted instruction.

However, the conclusions of researchers Douglas Marston and colleagues were restrained and "conservative" even for the impact of these leading instructional interventions because the "treatment outcomes were modest and inconsistent across models." "We were disappointed," they acknowledged, "that our data did not provide more evidence of robust effects for these approaches advocated in current research literature." Lesser and disappointing results from the heavy-phonics, skills-emphasis teaching is certainly not what a reader of the Report would ever learn to have been the actual results of this study.[26]

East St. Louis

East St. Louis in the early 1970s was the setting for another study with at-risk students who had used the phonics program Reading Mastery (Distar) in kindergarten through third grade. Another group used the same program, but not until first grade. A third group "received the district's traditional curriculum," which the researchers did not describe in any other way.[27] When the students were in ninth grade, Russell Gersten and his colleagues did follow-up testing and found that reading scores were higher for the children who had started the phonics program in kindergarten, and that both phonics groups outperformed the children who were taught only with the "traditional curriculum."

We could easily conclude from this study that if a school does use Reading Mastery, children would benefit most if the program were to begin in kindergarten rather than in first grade. The fundamental question, however, is whether this study, with its foil instruction of an undescribed "traditional curriculum," demonstrates that a heavy phonics program is the instruction of choice? The researchers themselves refrained from making this claim, concluding, "In no way do these quasi-experimental studies formally 'prove'" that Reading Mastery "is superior to other approaches."[28]

> *A shallow analysis that purports to inform public policy runs through the Report.*

Conducted in East St. Louis about thirty years ago, with its considerable methodological limitations, this study's inclusion in the Report, without context or historical perspective, is another stark example of the shallow analysis that purports to inform public policy. A national report that would seriously address the educational needs of poor, urban children would have to ask, What does this study really tell us about reading education and achievement in East St. Louis? Can we conclude that Reading Mastery or similar programs could possibly provide an answer to the educational needs of children in this city? If this were so, how can we explain that in 1997, approximately twenty-five years after this "successful" instruction, and nearly ten years after the publication of the investigation, 66 percent of the city's students failed the state's reading test? Is this because the city's educators were oblivious to a solution that was right under their noses?[29]

Of course any diligent panel's analysis of student failure in East St. Louis would know that national policy had to be informed by an examination of the social context—described vividly by Jonathan Kozol in his book *Savage Inequalities*—that went beyond the kind of magic bullet, stand-alone instructional view that fills the Report. As an urban area in which "75 percent of its population lives on welfare, the U.S. Department of Housing and Urban Development called East St. Louis 'the most distressed small city in America.'" Its children's well-being is assaulted by chemical plants that release toxins into the sewer system, by open sewers that convey toxic dumping, and by hazardous-waste incineration emissions that contaminate the city's air with heavy metal emissions, including lead, which are known to cause serious developmental and neurological problems in children. East St. Louis leads all other cities in Illinois in premature births. The average daily food expenditure is $2.40 per child. The schools are underfunded in relation to their children's extensive needs. Kozol writes, "In view of the extraordinary miseries of life for children" in the schools, the city "should be spending far more than is spent in wealthy suburbs." Yet the "city spends approximately half as much" per pupil "as the state's top-spending districts."[30] Staying true to the confined course the NRP had set for itself, the Report has nothing to say about any of this in relation to learning to read.

The Report could have done poor children an immeasurable service by telling Congress that "scientific research" reveals that for federal reading policy to be effective, sound reading instruction is necessary but not sufficient for helping these children learn to read.

"A Child-Aware Teacher"

The final study I will examine in this chapter taught beginning readers "onset and rime" units (e.g., *p-at, r-at, s-at*) for a month and concluded that the method was "effective" in assisting "children as they move into reading."[31] This is not really news because teachers have included these units, more traditionally known as word families (e.g., *dad, mad, lad, gad*), in reading instruction for ever and ever, and no instructional approach has ever excluded them. Considering how widely held this knowledge is in reading education, a brief summary of its reiteration in this study could end here.

However, the study is worth a closer look because it provides another view of the Report's one-track bias. Researchers Margareth Peterson and Leonard Haines addressed the question of how this kind of "onset and rime" instruction should be "delivered within the classroom context," that is, they posed the question of how skills should be taught. The researchers answered their question by rejecting "direct instruction" and instead recommended that teachers teach this skill when they see that a child is ready to learn it. They suggest that the "child-aware teacher," that is, a teacher who identifies a child's needs and addresses those needs when they arise, would teach the skill within a "contextual demonstration" at "opportune times, with opportune materials, in natural settings." By teaching this way, the researchers continued, the teacher would assist the learner in acquiring the "strategy as one ingredient in the *complex repertoire of knowledge, skills, and strategies that combine to promote literacy acquisition.*"[32] None of this is in the Report.

> Systematic phonics teaching is not superior to whole language teaching or teaching phonics as needed.

Conclusion

The review of the studies on phonics, in the previous chapter and this one, demonstrates that the Report's claims are not supported by what it points to as proof for its position. Systematic phonics training is not proven superior to whole language teaching or to teaching phonics as needed. Phonics training is not shown to provide special benefit to at-risk students. Overall, contrary to the Report's assertion, the "facts" should not persuade educators and the public about the purported value of systematic phonics instruction. Additional evidence for my appraisal can be found in the Appendix. The Report does provide evidence that phonics training is better than "no phonics instruction," but this straw man comparison, as I have repeatedly discussed, addresses a nonissue in the debate over phonics.[33]

The consequences of not having at least one beginning reading teacher on the NRP are probably nowhere more evident than in the Report's review of this research. To believe that by recommending the inclusion of phonics in instruction, especially with poor children, at-risk children, and so on, one contributes a needed scientific finding unknown to teachers is a naivete that can, at best, be the result of an absence of professional experience. Actually mandating it, in federal education legislation, as the sesame to these children's reading success goes far beyond naivete in the harm it surely will do them.

7 Encouraging Students to Read More

Especially odd is the Report's section on "Encouraging Students to Read More." Here the Report suddenly changes from allowing easy passage to any and all studies in the "Alphabetics" section that "support" a priori assumptions, to applying an intensive scrutiny to studies on another instructional practice. This practice, about which "there has been widespread agreement," the Report explains, is "encouraging children to read a lot." But, the Report soberly cautions, even though there "are few ideas more widely accepted . . . there could be a problem with this widespread belief." Did this practice really help make children "better readers"? asks the Report. Although "there seems little reason to reject the idea that lots of silent reading would provide students with valuable practice" to enhance fluency and comprehension, where, the Report wonders, is the evidence? Teachers might believe that encouraging students to "read more" contributes to reading achievement, but the NRP was not taking this for granted. Instead, rather than accepting a practice that seems self-evident, it was going to provide "a research synthesis of empirical studies that have tested

> The Report concludes that there is "not adequate evidence" to support "encouraging children to read a lot."

the efficacy of encouraging reading in terms of its impact on improving reading achievement."[1]

After ignoring the difference between causation and correlation throughout its "Alphabetics" section, the Report suddenly brings all its attention to this distinction. Yes, there are countless correlational studies suggesting a link between volume of reading and reading achievement; however, the Report admonishes, "correlations do not imply causation." Perhaps those students who read more do so because they are better readers and therefore choose to read. "Well," the Report ruminates, "it is impossible to know from correlational studies alone." Hence, the Panel probed the research databases for studies focused strictly on causation.[2]

At the end of its evaluation, the Report rejects orthodox thinking. "Despite widespread acceptance of the idea that schools can successfully encourage students to read more and that these increases in reading practice will be translated into better fluency and higher reading achievement," the Report concludes, "there is not adequate evidence to sustain this claim." And in case this statement were in any way ambiguous, the Report stresses that "it would be unreasonable to conclude that research shows that encouraging reading has a beneficial effect on reading achievement."[3]

In this chapter and the Appendix, I review the studies that the Report used for its appraisal. Because there is much to say about these studies, I have included in the chapter as many specifics as are necessary for supporting key observations; to avoid making the chapter overly—and tediously—detailed, I have put the rest in the Appendix.

"The Most Successful Method"

How did sustained silent reading (SSR), that is, silent reading of a book, magazine, or newspaper of the student's own choosing, compare with three kinds of programmed, independent reading instruction that required answers to comprehension questions? JoAnne Burley studied this question with "educationally and economically disadvantaged" high school students in a six-week summer program that included seventy-five minutes of daily reading instruction.[4] At the end of that time, reading comprehension scores were statically significant in favor of the SSR group, leading Burley to conclude that of the four groups, it was "the most successful method of reading practice used to improve literal and inferential reading comprehension, and fast reading for high school students considered to be educationally disadvantaged."[5]

Describing this study, the Report acknowledges the "positive, statistically significant difference favoring SSR over the other procedures on reading comprehension" but calls the difference "small."[6] This term is surprising because one would think that a "small" statistically significant improvement would have encouraged the use of SSR, even while calling for further research.

Replying to a letter by Stephen Krashen in *Education Week* that criticized the Report's appraisal of the SSR research, Timothy Shanahan, cochair of the NRP subcommittee on the SSR research, offered several defenses of the Report's interpretations. With respect to the Burley study, Shanahan claimed that its "students were not randomly assigned to the groups."[7] But contrary to Shanahan's claim, the Burley paper clearly states: "All students were randomly assigned to one of the four reading practice groups."[8]

Shanahan further downplayed the study by maintaining that "each of the four treatments was offered by a different teacher."[9] In fact, the Burley paper states: "The reading staff" was "randomly assigned to one of the four groups" and the "treatments all involved independent reading, not teacher-led instruction."[10]

Shanahan's last defense is ironic because had the Panel used this new standard that the benefits of teaching methods cannot be determined when each is instructed by a different teacher, the Panel would have had a scarcity of studies to use for the Report!

"More Positive About Reading"

A comparison of two groups of junior high school students, one of which used SSR and another that did not, extended over three years. The Report summarizes the comparative outcomes as showing "no differences" in reading achievement, an outcome that appears to support the Report's conclusions.[11]

Omitted from this summary, however, is any hint of the chief intention of this investigation. Because of the concern

Students who read independently "were more positive about the importance of reading."

many junior high school teachers have about a "falling off" of their
students' "reading habits and interests" during these school years,
researchers Ruth Cline and George Kretke wanted to see the possible impact of SSR on "students' attitudes toward reading."[12]

Their study found that compared to students who did not par-
ticipate in SSR programs, those who did "were more positive about
the importance of reading," were "more positive about reading a
book that they chose," "felt happier about going to the school
library," and "felt better about doing assigned reading." The
researchers concluded that while the "study showed no effect of
SSR on reading achievement," the significant differences in "attitudes" about reading were "encouraging tangible evidence to support the provision of reading practice time for students on a
continuous basis."[13]

This finding raises a critical question about the definition of
reading achievement. As the Report defines it, the term refers only
to what students do when reading—decoding, recognizing words,
and, very seldom, comprehending—and attitude is excluded. As the
concerns that produced this study suggest, however, other educators
have a more inclusive definition of reading achievement than that
which guided the Report. For them, "attitude toward reading" is an
integral part of reading achievement because students should
achieve, through reading education, a desire to read that helps pro-
pel their early learning and continues through their later grades into
adulthood. By arbitrarily—that is, without any empirical evidence—
excluding attitude from the definition of reading achievement, the
Panel not only reinforced its mechanical definition of reading
achievement but excluded essential information for determining the
value of the various facets of reading instruction.

"Statistically Significant" Rate Difference

In another study, second- through fourth-grade students used SSR for
fifteen weeks, ten to thirty minutes a day, while other students
engaged in spelling and English. No significant differences were
found in vocabulary or comprehension tests between the two groups.

The Report accurately conveys these results but is misleading in
describing the rate at which the SSR students moved through their
basal readers as only "slightly faster."[14] In fact, researcher Cathy

Collins reported that the rate difference between the groups was highly "statistically significant (.0005)" even though both "groups spent an equal amount of time in basal reader instruction."[15] A reader of the "Alphabetics" section of the Report will be challenged to find this degree of statistical significance favoring PA or phonics training described as "slightly" better.

The study also found that SSR contributed to considerable information for teachers that could be important for instruction. For example, teachers whose students engaged in SSR had a significantly greater awareness (.0001) of their students' specific reading interests. These teachers also recalled more "verbal responses that the students made concerning materials they had read (.0001)."[16]

"13 Percentiles Greater"

Mixed achievement results were found in this entire school year study of two eighth-grade classrooms, one of which devoted 80 percent of its reading instruction time to sustained silent reading, while the other devoted that percentage of time to reading that was teacher-directed and -monitored.

Because of attrition among the low-ability readers, only the outcomes of medium- and high-ability readers were reported. No differences were found for the high-ability readers, but the medium-ability students in the SSR class had significantly better reading test scores. Zaphaniah Davis explained that "average achievement" for the latter readers was "13 percentiles greater than was the directed reading activity class."[17]

The sudden hypercriticism of empirical research should have emerged in the Report's "Alphabetics" section.

Does this study encourage the use of SSR? The Report minimizes its import by raising a number of questions about the methodology: "How big were the initial differences across the groups?" "Was heterogeneity tested?"[18] Similarly, Shanahan complained about the "small sample size," unclear criterion for dividing students by ability, and other aspects of the study.[19] While these are very legitimate questions about any such research, it is unfortunate that this flourish of hypercriticism of empirical procedures and research design did not emerge earlier, in the "Alphabetics" section of the Report.

"Scored Significantly Higher"

Seventh- and eighth-grade children, predominantly black and poor, and reading two or more years below grade level, were in a ten-week study that added SSR to basal reading program textbooks and workbooks. One group reduced the instruction time by twenty minutes, three times a week, and read silently books and periodicals that were below their reading level. The other group continued working with the basal readers during this time. At the end of ten weeks, Sandra Holt and Frances O'Tuel found that there were no group differences in reading comprehension, but the seventh-grade SSR group "scored significantly higher on measures of reading vocabulary, and attitudes toward reading" and the eighth-grade experimental group had superior outcomes on vocabulary and two writing measures.[20] Neither the outcomes in writing nor the outcomes in attitude are mentioned in the Report's summary.

There is the usual "compared with what?" problem in this study, but with regard to the Report, which ignored this problem, the results are another instance of data that do not support the Report's conclusions about SSR.

.001 = "Small"

Another study that added SSR to a basal reading program evaluated six months' outcomes for a group of fifth and sixth graders who were reading books for thirty minutes each day and another group "involved in varied activities focusing on health, manners, and grooming."[21] On a reading achievement test, the difference favored the SSR group and was highly significant (.001).

NRP member Shanahan acknowledged that the Report's summary of the study was erroneous.

Inexplicably, the Report describes the difference as "small in terms of educational importance"—again, a description of that level of significance unseen in the "Alphabetics" section.[22] In a separate analysis, Stephen Krashen calculated the effect size for the SSR group to be "quite large (1.0005)."[23] The Report's description is especially curious because the results were for word reading, the level that the NRP model considers fundamental in building reading achievement.

Shanahan acknowledged, in his reply to Krashen, that the Report's summary was erroneous, but he explained that it occurred because the Panel made "no attempt to thoroughly analyze each study." Instead, he explained, it was the "overall quality of research" that the NRP considered: "the major findings, design features, strengths or weaknesses."[24] However since the Panel conducted effect size analyses for all of the "Alphabetics" studies, this description of the NRP's sudden alternative appraisal with these studies is not especially compelling.

Finally, this study all too obviously suffers from the "compared with what?" problem. However, this is never mentioned either in the Report or by Shanahan.

The Benefit of Peer Interaction

Three models of SSR were used with fourth graders for an entire school year. One group of students selected their own materials and read silently for thirty minutes, as did the teacher, who served as a role model. A second group did similar reading but added peer interaction centered on what the students were reading. The third group read silently and also had individual conferences with their teacher.

Researchers Gary Manning and Maryann Manning found that the peer interaction group made significantly greater gains in both reading attitude and achievement. The teacher conference group made a significant gain in attitude but not achievement.

Once again, restraint colors the Report's description: "when SSR was coupled with teacher conferences or peer discussion, then slight improvement was evident for the SSR groups" in reading achievement.[25] Reading the Report and without looking at the study itself, a reader would never know that this "slight improvement" for the peer interaction group was very statistically significant (at the .01 level) over the "other three groups."[26] Krashen also did an effect size calculation and found that between the peer interaction group and the control group, there was an above-a-medium-effect-size level (.57). This level is greater than "slight" even by the Panel's definitions of effect sizes. The peer interaction group had a similar statistically superior outcome on a measure of attitude, a finding the Report does not mention.

With respect to reading achievement alone, the Report is correct in its conclusion that "reading alone might provide no clear benefit but that additional reading in combination with other activities could be effective."[27] However, a panel that was open to a full exploration of the value of silent reading would at least have looked at other successful activities teachers have used for silent reading in their classes. The NRP did not.

Increase in "Children's Selection of Literature"

In a program that encouraged reading and enjoyment of books during "free-choice time," sixth graders could choose to read in the library center or do other activities, such as math games or arts and crafts. Researchers Lesley Morrow and Carol Weinstein found that although the program did not produce significant increases in reading achievement, "voluntary use of the library center" and "children's selection of literature" increased significantly both for high and low achievers. "These findings have direct implications for classroom instruction," the researchers concluded. "They document the behavioral changes that can occur when teachers carry out literature activities designed to increase interest in books."[28]

72 Versus 42 Total Points

Two of the studies used a computer-assisted program called Accelerated Reader (AR). Students actually read books and used the computer program to test themselves on each book read and to acquire points in an incentive system based both on the level of the book and on the tests the students successfully completed. The program can be criticized for its relentless testing program, its superficial, multiple-choice comprehension measures, its incentive system that undermines the development of intrinsic motivation to read, and so forth. In order to provide a consistent evaluation of the Report, however, I will put these criticisms aside and accept the definition of AR as another form of sustained silent reading and the Report's inclusion of this study in the SSR pool.

In this investigation, students who used the AR program from fourth through eighth grade were compared with other students who, instead of using the AR program, were engaged in conventional teacher-directed reading and language arts instruction. At the end of five years, Janie Peak and Mark Dewalt found that the mean gain for the AR students was 72 total points on a standardized reading test, compared with 42 total points for the control group.[29] Moreover, the AR program students had lower average reading test scores than the controls when the study began at the end of third grade, but higher test scores when the study concluded at the end of eighth grade!

The Report concludes that because this study had "problematic" test score calculations and "limited data" about what the control group "students were doing" during the experimental time, "it is unclear whether any real difference in achievement can be attributed" to this free-reading program.[30] These are justifiable concerns, but it is peculiar to see a complaint about "limited data" emerging at this point in the Report.

Importance of Reading "Connected Text"

Is comprehension a holistic process from which individual skills cannot be extracted and isolated, or is it composed of distinct skills? The question is an important one because if the answer is, or leans toward, a holistic process, that would give greater support to time spent in independent, silent reading of whole texts, an activity in which the reader engages numerous, integrated facets of comprehension. If, on the other hand, the answer is, or leans toward, the distinct skills explanation, that would support more teacher-directed instruction of separate skills.

To address the question, Ray Reutzel and Paul Hollingsworth divided fourth- and sixth-grade students into several skills-instruction groups who were taught ten lessons in one of the following: locating details; drawing conclusions; identifying a story sequence; or determining the main idea.[31] Representing the holistic view was a group engaged in sustained silent reading of literature books during the time the four treatment groups received skills instruction. The ten sessions, approximately thirty minutes each, continued over a month's time.

The study's results did not show that skills instruction was superior to SSR in promoting comprehension.

At the end of that time, as the Report states, there were "no reading differences" among the groups on tests of the skills that were taught, which for the Report implies that SSR had no superior value. This was not, however, what the researchers found or concluded. Their research supported the view that comprehension is a "unitary skill or process rather than a set of discrete skills or subskills which can be taught one at a time." Contrary to the skills-emphasis view, the results did not show that skills instruction was superior to sustained silent reading in promoting comprehension. The results of the study, the researchers proposed, "argue for a unitary or holistic view of reading comprehension and one which emphasizes the importance of engaging in reading of connected text as a primary means for improvement of reading comprehension"![32]

"Statistically Significant Increase"

The other Accelerated Reader research in the SSR pool of investigations was a two-part study with "severely socio-economically disadvantaged" sixth graders. In the first part, Stacy Vollands and colleagues found that the AR group "showed a statistically significant increase" on two tests of reading comprehension and one of reading accuracy, but the comparison group did not.[33] On measures of attitude toward reading, the "AR girls showed statistically significantly better attitudes toward reading than the boys," who demonstrated no group difference. The Report dourly describes this study as showing "a small advantage" for the AR group and does not report the attitude outcomes.[34]

The second part of the study was, as both the original researchers and the Report note, poorly conducted: reading time was not controlled, the student groups were not well matched, the control group also had silent reading time, and so forth. Nonetheless, the Report misrepresents the outcomes. For example, on one reading comprehension test, the published study states, the "AR group showed a very large statistically significant increase from a lower baseline" while the control group "showed a small decrease."[35] On the reading attitude survey, the girls in the AR group had statistically better scores in reading attitudes.

> *Eight of the fourteen studies showed that SSR groups made superior gains in reading achievement.*

These results do not translate into the Report's summary that "there was not" an advantage for AR instruction.[36]

Connecting Correlational and Causal Findings

A tally of the cumulative results of these studies reveals that eight of the fourteen studies showed that the SSR groups made superior gains in reading achievement in areas such as comprehension, word recognition, vocabulary, and amount of work covered in a reading textbook. Within these eight studies there were approximately a dozen significant outcomes favoring SSR. Several studies showed benefits in attitudes toward reading; no study showed a decline in attitude or motivation. Additional contributions of SSR were identified, such as increasing teachers' awareness of students' specific reading interests. Those studies that achieved positive results in a relatively short to moderate amount of time with poor readers in the middle and upper grades seem especially praiseworthy.

These results do not provide sufficient evidence for a decisive conclusion about the value of SSR, but they do provide enough to cast serious doubt on the NRP judgment that it "would be unreasonable to conclude that research shows that encouraging reading has a beneficial effect on reading achievement."[37] There is something so blatantly and absurdly wrong with this statement and the Report's conclusions about SSR that it caused respected educators such as Lucy Calkins, founding director of the Teachers College Reading and Writing Project at Columbia University, to exclaim, "To question that reading makes you into a good reader, well, it seems to me they have lost their marbles to say that is just correlational."[38] The most informed judgment about the SSR studies should be that they offer sufficient evidence for educators to continue "encouraging reading," while at the same time continuing to pursue answers for how best to do it.

Several SSR studies showed benefits in attitudes toward reading.

These studies also need to be seen as bolstering the causal associations suggested in the correlational research. It is one thing not to confuse the two, but another to conceptualize these studies as though they were a handful of investigations isolated from all previous work, such as volume of reading. Summarizing this work, reading researcher Richard Allington concludes that "regardless of how volume of reading was measured, there exists a potent relationship between" it and reading achievement. He also cites his own studies, done over a decade, that have shown that "differences in the volume of classroom reading were associated with elementary students' reading achievement." Other studies too have concluded that the amount of classroom time spent reading is positively related to reading achievement and that struggling readers spend less time reading than do their higher-achieving peers. This is why Allington recommends allocating considerable time each classroom day to *actual reading*."[39]

Attitude

As I pointed out earlier, the Report's narrow definition of reading achievement is perhaps a major deficiency in judging the "impact" of SSR on "improving reading achievement."[40] Omitted in this judgment is a broader perspective of achievement found in the SSR research—a perspective that includes attitude—especially as it pertains to aliteracy, a term used to describe those who can read but choose not to. According to both a survey that has tracked the reading habits of Americans through the 1990s and a Gallup Poll, people are reading less and less. Educationally, as Jim Trelease, author of *The Read-Aloud Handbook*, put it, "you go through school having learned to read and then you leave school not wanting to read."[41]

> *Many researchers were concerned that the kind of skills instruction the Report advocates would diminish children's desire to read.*

Morrow and Weinstein, along with other SSR researchers and educators, expressed concern with the problem of aliteracy and the "substantial number of children [who] do not choose to read either for pleasure or for information." A possible source of this problem, they proposed, may be reading programs that are "skills-oriented and provide little opportunity for students to read for enjoyment." Or, putting this in terms of the Report, they were concerned that the kind of reading instruction the Report advocates is exactly the kind that would diminish children's desire to read. It was time, Morrow and Weinstein argued, "for schools to look beyond achievement test performance and to implement reading programs that include as a major purpose the development of voluntary reading."[42]

This brings us back to a question the Report chooses to ignore: Is enhancing children's enthusiasm and positive attitudes toward books a phenomenon that follows learning to read, or should it be part of learning to read, both to enhance that learning and to avert aliteracy? Again, through a decision for which no evidence was provided, the NRP chose the former model, leaving the issue and role of voluntary reading outside its vision of what constitutes sound reading instruction.

Why the Report Rejected SSR

What is really at issue in the Report's negative conclusion about "encouraging reading"? Part of it must stem from the Panel's antipathy to anything that veers away from its direct instruction model. Continuous, independent reading of books seems emblematic of literature-based/whole language teaching and carries a constructionist view of children's ability to solve problems encountered as they learn to read and write. It carries too a belief that direct teaching is not required for all the essentials children need to know. Independent reading reduces teacher control and makes students more active participants. These are qualities of silent reading that skills-emphasis proponents might very likely consider to be part of soft, feel-good, and wrongheaded (or -hearted) teaching.

It is these associations, I suggest, that have blinded the Report's appraisal of the SSR studies, their positive findings, and the connections between the correlational and causal research. It has led the Panel to be blind to educators' legitimate concerns about aliteracy, a blindness that has caused the NRP to recede into a foolish corner of not "encouraging" silent reading.

Silent Reading in Literature-Based Classes

I do recognize a legitimate concern suggested in the Report about some of the limits of silent reading, concerns that teachers themselves have had: Is a book too hard or easy for a student? Is the book contributing to a student's reading growth? What does a student do

> *The Panel kept itself from pursuing vital questions about how to incorporate silent reading into sound instruction.*

when he or she comes to unknown words, vocabulary, and concepts? How does a teacher know if a student is comprehending a book? How does a teacher know if the student is faking reading?

Certainly there is nothing in sustained silent reading, independent of a sound reading program and an array of supports, related activities, and oversight, that guarantees a positive contribution to reading growth. However, in the blindness to which I have pointed, the Panel kept itself from pursuing vital questions about how to incorporate silent reading into sound instruction.

In her book *On Solid Ground: Strategies for Teaching Reading K–3*, Sharon Taberski observes that in her *literature-based classroom*, "just sending [students] off to read independently doesn't necessarily provide the kind of practice they need."[43] Similarly, "literature-based, workshop-oriented" educators Ellen Oliver Keene and Susan Zimmermann expressed concern that during silent reading "many children are not so engaged as they read. They don't know when they're comprehending. They don't know when they're not, they don't know whether it's critical for them to comprehend a given piece. And if they don't comprehend, they don't know what to do about it."[44]

They also recognized that teachers should not assume that oral reading sufficiently prepares students for silent reading: "We

> *Silent reading should be part of a reading curriculum but could benefit from some instructional supports and enhancements.*

watched many [students] struggle to understand and then discuss what they read. Most were competent oral readers. They pronounced words correctly, missed few words, and sounded out words they didn't know. But many were so disconnected from the meaning of the text, especially expository text, that they were often unaware of the essence of what they were reading."[45]

Observations such as these lead to an awareness that silent reading should be an essential part of a reading curriculum but could benefit from some instructional supports and enhancements. In various ways, "explicit instruction in reading expository text would be critical," these literature-based educators concluded, and they pursued several means of providing it.[46]

For example, one way to alert a teacher to the difficulties students are experiencing during silent reading is by using yellow self-adhesive notes (Post-it Notes). On them the children employ various codes, such as a question mark for a word or part of the text they did not understand, and the codes provide information for the teacher's future reading conferences with each student. In these conferences the teacher asks the child "to describe his or her thinking at the time the note was placed in the text." The teacher can also use the notes to assess the children's "comprehension and develop a plan for the next day."[47]

Silent reading can be promoted not only through teacher-student interactions but through interactions among students in the kind of mutual work found effective in one study (but described in the Report as sullying the results of "pure" SSR). Students meet in small groups or pairs to discuss "what is most important in the text and how they came to that conclusion." Book clubs discuss the important conclusions each member might have drawn from a book. "By asking children to share what worked in their reading," says Taberski, "I'm helping them transform what was effective *once* into a strategy to apply to new situations. I'm also asking them to take a metacognitive stance—to look at and evaluate what they do as they read so that they can do more of what's working and less of what isn't. This way, children begin to acquire a repertoire of strategies to employ at will. They know there are techniques they can try and approaches they can use to get better."[48]

In these illustrations, we see literacy instruction that encourages, supports, and advances independent silent reading—conceives of silent reading within a totality of reading instruction—that is far different from the Report's narrow conception of SSR. Regrettably, the Report's conclusions have been echoed in many influential places. The American Federation of Teachers, for example, stated, "The panel found no positive relationship between programs and instruction that encourage large amounts of independent silent reading and improvements in reading achievement."[49] And *Education Week* reported, "it could not be determined from the available research whether [silent reading] actually improves reading skills."[50] These echoes can only confuse teachers and the public, help eliminate good teaching practices, and foster aliteracy. Writer Elizabeth Hardwick wrote, "The greatest gift is the passion for reading. It is cheap, it consoles, it distracts, it excites, it gives you knowledge of the world and experience of a wide kind. It is a moral illumination." Thanks to "scientific reading instruction," children will be moving away from that deeper meaning of reading achievement as fast as the skills can carry them.

8 Unhandcuffing Reading Education

The Texas "Miracle"

An adequate understanding of the National Reading Panel Report and the Bush reading legislation requires placing them within the context of Bush's educational and social policies both in Texas and the White House. According to NRP member Sally Shaywitz and her husband and coresearcher, Bennett A. Shaywitz, Bush's initial policy steps were thorough and scholarly: he and Reid Lyon "looked first to the science, to the empirical data and based on that evidence, developed proposals for more effective approaches to teaching reading."[1] Surely the two of them huddled studiously over the data would have been a sight to behold. Lacking that, we are left only with the practical results accrued in subsequent steps, chief of which is the "Texas educational miracle" Bush was supposed to have spearheaded as governor from 1994 to 2000. A brief examination of this "miracle" is worthwhile because it provides an informed picture of extensive educational outcomes that skills-emphasis reading instruction has produced and is likely to produce for the nation.

A "Bush for President" news release boasted that "reading performance in Texas has improved since Bush became governor: 88 percent of the third-grade students passed the reading portion of the state assessment test in 1999—up from 76 percent in 1994." Minority students too were described as having "made strong gains" on the state's own Texas Assessment of Academic Skills (TAAS). For example, "African-American students in both the eighth and fourth grade increased their passing rate on the reading exam by 23 points between 1994 and 1999."[2]

Discussing "Reading: The Key to Success," Laura Bush praised her husband's educational successes. "When Governor Bush took office," she said, "one in five Texas school children was failing the reading portion of the state's skills test. To change this disturbing statistic," he and the education commissioner "laid out a plan to equip every child in Texas with essential skills for learning" and thereby "ensure that every child in Texas learns to read by the third grade and continues reading at grade level or better throughout his or her public school years." According to Mrs. Bush, "The plan is working. Texas public schools are improving. Test scores continue to climb, and minority student achievement is the best we've seen in decades."[3]

Similarly praised were the reported educational achievements under Rod Paige, the superintendent of the Houston schools before he became secretary of education in the Bush administration. The *New York Times*, for example, reported that under Paige, Houston schools had "improved reading scores."[4] Presumably, this was one reason that, shortly before becoming secretary of education, Paige received the Harold W. McGraw Jr. (of McGraw-Hill publishers) $25,000 Prize in Education.[5]

"You teach a child to read, and he or her will be able to pass the literary test," Bush explained.

What was the formula for the dramatic improvements in performance on the Texas tests? In the second month of his presidency, George W. Bush provided a succinct answer: "You teach a child to read, and he or her will be able to pass the literary test."[6]

Texas Myth

The chief problem with Bush's syllogism is not its misuse of grammar and words—*her* for *she* and *literary* for *literacy*—but its logic. Yes, if children genuinely learn to read, they will most likely be able to pass a literacy test; however, the converse is not necessarily true: if students pass a literacy test (e.g., the TAAS), that does not necessarily reveal their reading abilities. Similarly, the cumulative pass rates on the TAAS do not necessarily demonstrate a Texas miracle.

The "Texas miracle" was actually the "Texas myth." Reading scores have been no better than the national average.

The work of educational researcher Walt Haney, comparing the TAAS scores with those of Texas students' performance on the National Assessment of Educational Progress (NAEP), contains evidence of this syllogistic non sequitur and for Haney's conclusion that the "Texas miracle" was actually the "Texas myth." He found that the seemingly huge overall achievement gains demonstrated on the TAAS were not duplicated on the latter, nonpartisan measure. For example, the performance of Texas fourth and eighth graders during the Bush years was "very similar to the performance of fourth- and eighth-graders nationally," just as it had been before he took office. Haney found "not a single instance in which average NAEP scores in Texas vary from national means by as much as two-tenths of a standard deviation."[7] For example, fourth-grade reading for Texas in 1998 was a mean of 217, exactly the same as the national average on the reading test at fourth grade. The 1998 eighth-grade reading score mean was 262 for students in Texas, compared

Between 1992 and 1998 the reading score gap has increased between white and minority fourth-grade students in Texas.

with 264 for students nationally. For minority students, contrary to claims about the racial achievement gap narrowing in Texas, outcomes were worse. Between 1992 and 1998, the NAEP reading scores for fourth graders showed an increase in the gap between white and minority students.[8]

Why have students done better on the Texas Assessment of Academic Skills than on national tests? Interviews with teachers, Haney reported, suggest that teaching to the test was a large part of the answer: Classes have emphasized teaching TAAS-related content while deemphasizing content not related to the test. As added insurance, "in most schools TAAS practice quizzes were administered on a regular basis with emphasis on teaching to the TAAS format, such as having students practice 'bubbling' in answers on machine scorable answer sheets."[9]

Rice University educational researcher Linda McNeil has concluded that many students pass the TAAS reading tests "by being able to select among answers given; they are not able to read assignments, to make meaning of literature, to complete reading assignments outside of class."[10] McNeil also laments that "instead of reading novels, kids are skimming three-paragraph passages for key words."[11]

McNeil and University of Texas at Austin Professor Angela Valenzuela found that "the TAAS emphasis on reading short passages, then selecting among answers given to questions based on those short passages, has made it very difficult for students to read a sustained reading assignment." With respect to the "fourth-grade slump," middle school teachers report that after several years of work with TAAS practice materials, middle school students often are "unable to read a novel even two years below grade level."[12]

Supporting Haney's conclusions about student achievement in Texas is a RAND study by Stephen Klein and colleagues, which also compared the scores on the TAAS with those on the NAEP for fourth and eighth graders.[13] Summing up their findings on the "Texas miracle," Klein said, "It's not a miracle. We think these [TAAS] scores are misleading and biased because they're inflated. They're improvements in scores, but not in proficiency."[14]

Of the fifteen cities with the highest dropout rates during Bush's years as governor, six were in Texas.

Neither did Haney find evidence that beginning reading and unceasing testing produced any long-term educational miracle. Texas, throughout Bush's governorship, had been among the top states in high school dropout rates, especially for black students, whose graduation rate under Bush was about 60 to 65 percent, well below the national average of 82 percent.[15] A study by Robert Balfanz and Nettie Legters of the Center for Social Organization of Schools at Johns Hopkins University supported Haney's dropout conclusions. They found that of the fifteen cities with the highest dropout rates, six were in Texas (San Antonio, Fort Worth, Dallas, Houston, Austin, and El Paso) during Bush's years as governor. Former Superintendent Rod Paige's school system, Houston, had the seventh-highest dropout rate among the nation's urban school districts, with fewer than 50 percent of freshmen graduating four years later.[16]

Texas Education Facts

The Bush "signature issue" is, in fact, a simplistic—and wholly inadequate—bootstrap solution to the education of children, especially poor children. Instead of focusing on a well-trained, professionally competent teaching force and on providing it with all that is required to ensure a rich education for children, he supports scientific reading education that offers seemingly "teacher-proof" packaged programs. The Bush approach provides education-on-the-cheap while enhancing the profits of publishers like McGraw-Hill, the major producer of the packaged programs.

One example of Bush's indifference to building a professional, experienced teaching force is Texas teachers' salaries, which under his governorship ranked thirty-sixth among the states. One study found that 28 percent of Texas teachers had to take second jobs.[17] Although Bush frequently mentions giving the teachers a $3,000 pay raise in 1999, the largest in fifteen years, he leaves out the fact that he fought for a $1,500 raise but lost to the Democrats, who had first proposed a $6,000 pay raise.[18]

Bush attempted to take credit for some educational reforms that preceded his tenure as governor. For instance, reduced class size reform that included a mandatory maximum of twenty-two students per class from kindergarten through fourth grade was established by Democratic Governor Mark White in 1984. Yet even while associating himself with this reform, after becoming governor, Bush "called for effectively eliminating the limit on class size," saying it was "an infringement of local control."[19] Under Bush, the number of schools requesting and receiving class-size waivers (allowing them to increase class size) increased.[20]

Campaigning as a strong supporter of education when he first ran for governor, Bush pledged to increase the state's share of public school funding from 45 percent to 60 percent. Yet when Bush left office, the Texas Legislative Budget Board reported, the state's share of public school funding had fallen to 44 percent, the lowest percentage since the state began educational reform in 1984.[21]

Bush showed no meaningful concern for the various aspects of children's lives that influence learning success or failure.

Bush's signature issue also masks his overall colossal indifference to children. While proclaiming a dedication to ensuring that children obtain basic reading skills—a far cry from ensuring a full education—he showed no meaningful concern for children's living conditions and overall quality of their lives, elements with incalculable effects on learning success or failure. For example, Texas ranked second among states in the percentage of people—especially children—who went hungry and third in the percentage of malnourished citizens. After Bush vetoed a bill to coordinate hunger programs in Texas, reporters asked him about hunger in the state. "Where?" was his reply.[22]

Under Bush, Texas was tied for the third highest percentage of children in poverty. Just three states provided lower welfare help. Under Bush, Texas slashed its food stamp payments, an essential program for the poorest of children, by $1 billion. Also under Bush, Texas ranked second in the percentage of poor children who lacked health insurance.[23] In 1999, when Texas was flush with a budget surplus, Bush initially fought to block some 250,000 children from receiving affordable health care. While fighting this insurance program, he declared a legislative emergency to push through a $45 million tax break for oil well owners, saying, "People are hurting out there." He also had the opportunity to invest more of the surplus in education but instead pursued tax cuts.[24]

President Bush

As Bush carried his Texas game plan into the White House, accolades for his educational budget and dedication to education were ceaseless, with few commentators bothering to investigate beyond the facade.

What exactly was Bush's budgetary great leap forward, for example? Had he gotten his way, his increase in the education budget of approximately $2.5 billion for fiscal year 2002 would have been about 5.9 percent. In contrast, the fiscal year 2001 education budget, the last Clinton budget, was $42.1 billion, an increase of 18 percent over the previous year's funding. The final budget that Bush signed, following revisions in the House and Senate, was $48.9 billion, an increase of approximately 16.2 percent—not an insignifi-

"We really thought if [Bush] were serious about education, [he] would give us somewhere close to the resources that are needed."

cant increase, but again, less than the last Clinton increase of 18 percent.[25] (The 48.9 billion is also about the same size as the increase Bush requested for the military budget shortly after signing the educational legislation.[26])

Although the budget put $900 million into promoting scientifically based reading education, other areas of education were cut and more cuts were planned. Support for libraries decreased, even in light of the documented substantial inequalities between classroom libraries in rich and poor school systems and despite strong documentation for the relationship between access to print and reading achievement. The cuts, an American Library Association executive calculated, could "buy nearly 1.1 million hardcover books," and, the executive added, "We really thought if they were serious about education, they would give us somewhere close to the resources that are needed."[27] The budget he submitted eliminated all funds for the National Writing Project, a program that promotes "professional development activities and programs that foster improvements in teaching and learning of writing" across the nation. Only because of an extensive campaign by the Project and its supporters were the funds restored and increased in the Bush budget. Nevertheless, shortly after signing the No Child Left Behind legislation in January 2002, Bush recommended eliminating funding for the National Writing Project and other "low-priority" education programs in the fiscal year 2003 budget![28]

During the Budget Committee's deliberations, the Democrats offered several amendments that would have provided additional funds critical for improving education, such as class-size reduction and school renovation and construction. The Republicans defeated all these amendments. Following his signing of the education legislation in January 2002, Bush also proposed cutting all funds for rural education, school counseling, and educational technology.[29] Barely enlarged were funds for Head Start, a 1.9 percent proposed increase that allowed the program simply to maintain its enrollment level of less than 50 percent of all children eligible for the program.[30]

Little attention was given to school conditions or to ensuring a professionally solid teaching force. For example, in Los Angeles, overcrowding has forced children to attend school on a staggered year-round schedule; half of all new teachers, and a quarter of all teachers, lack formal teaching credentials. Instead, Bush proposed freezing funds for teacher quality programs.[31]

At the same time, as organizations like the Children's Defense Fund document, approximately 12 million children—one in six— live in poverty. Although there was a recent drop in the poverty rate in 2001, children were more likely to be poor than they were twenty or thirty years before. The child poverty rate was highest for African Americans (30 percent) and Latinos (28 percent), but by international standards, it was also exceptionally high for white children (10 percent). For children under six, the "near poverty" rate was 40 percent![32]

Twelve million children were in households unable to afford adequate and nutritious food. About 3.6 million children lived in "severely substandard housing." Eleven million children had no health insurance and were "less likely to receive medical and dental care when they needed it" or have adequate follow-up care "to manage chronic illnesses like asthma or diabetes."[33]

Of course these conditions were not created by the Bush administration; nevertheless, it is within this context that Bush's compassion and concern for children must be judged. Even if his scientific reading education were actually to have a scientific basis, focusing on reading education alone, without concern for these catastrophic realities, would have to be seen in a questionable light. Instead, we can only conclude that the Bush reading education legislation, containing deficient solutions and false promises, is part and parcel of the rest of his policy of indifference to all but the wealthy.

> *For Bush, reading comprehension appears to mean recognizing the right and wrong answers.*

Bush and Reading

Reading instruction that minimizes actual reading and conceives of comprehension as recognizing the right and wrong answers to test questions appears to be consonant with the meaning of reading in Bush's personal development and current functioning as president. Despite claiming that reading education is his signature issue, and the <www.whitehousekids.gov> website listing reading as his top favorite pastime, George W. Bush's apparent aversion to reading is sufficiently well-known to inspire endless jokes, such as Paul Begala's, "Let's be honest. If you want to hide something from George

W. Bush, put it in a book,"[34] and Arianna Huffington's "uncurious George," a play on the title of the popular children's book series he consistently reads to young students.[35]

Whenever asked about his reading, his replies never inspire awe. "I can't remember any specific books," he told a child who asked him to name the book he liked most when he was young.[36] Asked the same question another time, he replied that it was *The Very Hungry Caterpillar*, even though the book was published in 1969, the year after Bush graduated from Yale.[37] When asked to name something at which he isn't good, he said, "Sitting down and reading a 500-page book on public policy or philosophy or something." He has also used joking, self-deprecating tactics to deflect criticism of his reading, such as "[Bill Buckley and I] go way back, and we have a lot in common. Bill wrote a book at Yale—I read one."[38]

Mark Crispin Miller, author of *The Bush Dyslexicon*, has provided a keen insight into Bush's views on reading comprehension, the purpose of reading books, and, indirectly, his emphasis on skills and testing. In a Republican candidates debate, when Bush was asked what lessons he had learned from a biography of Dean Acheson he said he had been reading, Bush gave a rambling answer that cobbled together snippets of speeches and contained not a single remark about the book itself. Responding to another question a few minutes later, Senator John McCain brought a portion of the Dean Acheson biography into his answer and even quoted an exchange Acheson had had with Harry Truman. Piqued by the speculation that he might not have read the book, Bush said about McCain's performance, "Maybe I should have picked out one little bitty detail of the book. I don't think so. I thought my answer was the right answer, otherwise I wouldn't have given it."[39]

Miller observes that Bush's "defensive self-appraisal" says it all, capturing what's wrong with his "way of reading" and "education plans." There could be no "right answer" to the open-ended question. Rather, the question offered Bush the opportunity to use this book about past foreign policy to think aloud about the foreign policy he envisioned. "But all that Bush could do was quickly rummage through his little bag of 'themes' for 'the right answer.'" He later told the *Washington Post* he had "absolutely hammered" the question, as if all that mattered was the right answer to an examination question. What mattered was not the ideas in the book, what they meant to him, and how they applied to the political issues that faced him and the nation, but only that he got a good score. Thus, if he had actually read the biography, Miller concludes, "he read it just as he has always read (or had his staffers read) the memos and reports that cross his desk: in search of simple, handy bits for later use. This is not the way to lead or read—or to teach children how to read."[40]

> *Reading for Bush is a utilitarian process of gathering together pieces of information for later performance.*

Could this add to the explanation of why Bush extols skills as he does, and of what appears to be the perfect fit between the skills-emphasis pedagogy and the reading education mandated in his legislation? Reading, for Bush, is not about extensive, deep comprehension, not about comprehension leading to possible transformation. Reading for him is a utilitarian process of gathering together pieces of information for later performance, rather than one that is connected to thinking, personal development, and application to a reader's life and world.

An encounter between Bush and children in a classroom provides a final insight into Bush's conception of reading instruction. According to journalist Arianna Huffington, since first running for governor, Bush has "made hundreds and hundreds of school appearances over the years and it's always the same drill: Anytime he gets within shouting distance of school kids, no matter their age—whoosh!—out comes *The Very Hungry Caterpillar*." Therefore, at an Albuquerque school, although the book is geared toward preschoolers, Bush read it to the second graders. "You could almost see the kids rolling their eyes in unison," Huffington says, "but Bush wasn't going to deviate from his historically narrow comfort zone, even though he admitted" afterward that the book was not age-appropriate: "These kids are way beyond *The Hungry Caterpillar*," he said.

Pondering why Bush "only feels comfortable reading the same children's book again and again," Huffington proposes, "It's what this confirms about him. After all, the essence of reading is encountering new ideas and different viewpoints, and here is a man who has no interest in either of these things." Reading for Bush is performance. It is not about engaging children's interest. It is not about generating a discussion. And it is not about associating children's experiences and previous ideas to their current comprehension of a book. Books seem to have as little place in learning to read as they do in Bush's life. Nonetheless, "I like to read. I read a lot," he told the Albuquerque students. When asked what he thought of a six hundred-plus-page biography of John Adams he was supposedly reading as part of his "typical" day, he answered, "I like it. It's interesting." About which Huffington remarked, "Well there you have it. Literary analysis worthy of the *Paris Review*."[41]

What "Science Tells Us"

As I was finishing this book, proclamations about the new scientifically based reading instruction were making headlines week after week. First Lady Laura Bush, for example, speaking before the House Education and Workforce Committee, insisted that there was no excuse for elementary school teachers not knowing how to teach children to read. "We now know—because science tells us—what teaching methods are most effective." Unlike the skills-emphasis scientists, however, the first lady accurately observed that it was traditional teaching, not any kind of new instruction, that this science claimed to validate. The fundamental message of this science was: let's get back to basics. Why? Because "the basics work," said Mrs. Bush. "Reading programs that include phonics and phonemic awareness work. Regular testing works. Some methods are tried and true, and we must make sure our teachers learn them."[42]

> *The phrase "science tells us" makes doctrine based on biased beliefs appear to be objective, independent findings based on impartial pursuits.*

The phrase "science tells us" is frequently heard among skills-emphasis proponents. Testifying before the House Committee on Education and the Workforce in 1999, Reid Lyon described what the "research has taught us."[43] The same committee heard Representative Anne Northup of Kentucky praise Bush's reading legislation because it was based on what "science tells us" about reading instruction.[44] And commenting on the contributions of the NRP Report "and Reid Lyon's energy and efforts," NRP member Sally Shaywitz and her husband, Bennett Shaywitz, enthused, "there is hope of closing the gap between what science tells us and what happens in the classroom."[45] The use of the phrase "what science tells us" is extraordinary insofar as it reconceptualizes what is no more than a doctrine based on biased beliefs into what is continually described as objective, independent findings based on impartial pursuits. Pure science conveys its truths to us: we tell it nothing; it "tells us." The phrase might not be a bad one if we were told the actual findings in this science.

In summing up, I want to reemphasize that this is not a debate about whether or not phonemic awareness, phonics, and other word skills contribute to learning to read. Everyone debating beginning reading education agrees that they do and that these skills should be taught. The question at issue is, How and to what extent should skills be taught, especially in relation to other strategies?

The debate is also not about whether direct, systematic, and explicit instruction should be part of teaching. Here, too, everyone agrees that it should be. The question is, How much and when should it be part of reading instruction?

Finally, the debate is not about whether scientific knowledge and empirical studies can contribute to formulating instruction. Rather, the questions are, What do the empirical studies actually show? What does scientific knowledge contribute? and, Is it sufficient for formulating instruction?

The studies used in the Report actually do help us clarify these issues. This science—in contrast to the Report's interpretation of this science—tells us that the claims that "PA training benefits . . . reading comprehension" and that "PA training improved children's ability to read . . . in the long term," as determined by tests of reading comprehension that "yielded statistically significant effect sizes" is simply not supported by the evidence in the studies reviewed in the Report. Neither is there evidence in these studies that PA training contributes a long-term reading benefit to children who are "at risk for developing reading problems in the future."[46]

Neither is there evidence that teaching PA skills in a direct, systematic training program is superior to teaching these skills as needed. The science shows us that if the skills are taught this way, beginning readers will learn them. However, the very science used in the Report also shows that the skills can also be taught as needed and within larger written language activities. That is, a teacher can identify specific skills that children need, teach those skills, and not bother to teach skills that children demonstrate they have already acquired. This would seem more efficient and the only concern would be whether a teacher is able to identify and teach all the specific skills needed in a full classroom of children.

The Report's studies do not justify mandating one approach over others.

This legitimate concern is allayed by the outcomes of the Report's studies that found that, according to reading outcome measures, teachers who taught this way were effective.

Neither did the studies used in the Report support the conclusion that "systematic phonics instruction makes a bigger contribution to children's growth in reading than alternative programs providing unsystematic" phonics instruction.[47] Hence, a reasonable conclusion, based on the Report's studies, should be a pro-choice one that allows teachers to choose the method of skills instruction they want to use. The Report's studies do not justify mandating one approach over others.

The studies comparing literature-based/whole language instruction with more direct forms of teaching also lead at least to a pro-choice conclusion. That is, strictly in terms of the outcome measures, both approaches are equally effective, and the science clearly does not support the conclusion that "phonics produced better reading growth" than "whole language approaches."[48] Looking solely at the NRP Report research, we can conclude, first, that a beginning reading approach that encourages the use of multiple strategies for identifying words and obtaining meaning is at least as effective, and can be even more effective, than one that encourages reliance primarily on phonemic and phonics skills strategies.

Again, any legislation and policy using the actual scientific findings of the Report's studies would, at a minimum, have to encourage a pro-choice position. Moreover, even within a pro-choice option, educators and the public would have to be cautioned that the scientific evidence for the long-term benefits of skills-emphasis, stepwise, direct instruction in beginning reading, especially at the cost of minimizing meaning and comprehension, is virtually nonexistent. What the science actually shows us is the necessity of basing reading instruction policy on more than the evidence from empirical studies.

The studies I have reviewed in the previous chapters constitute the fundamental evidence cited on behalf of the skills-emphasis, stepwise, small-to-large-parts reading instruction model recommended in the NRP Report and mandated in the Bush reading legislation and in other policy documents at state and local levels. I have not covered two sections on beginning reading instruction that are in the Report— one on guided oral reading and another on reading comprehension— because such a discussion would add nothing that would help us appraise it. The debate is not about whether comprehension should be part of beginning reading instruction. Rather, the issue is whether the model in the Report and legislation is correct: do children first have to go through a stepwise progression of basic skills before comprehension becomes a substantial part of instruction? The Report's section on reading comprehension offers a number of suggestions for teaching it but assumes that comprehension must stay in its place within the stepwise model, gaining serious attention only after the acquisition of a sequence of skills. The Report's research evidence offers no evidence to support this assumption.

> *Any legislation and policy using the actual scientific findings of the Report would, at a minimum, have to encourage a pro-choice position.*

Choice? No!

The fact that the Report's studies support, at the minimum, a pro-choice position is anathema to the skills-emphasis proponents. NICHD-supported researcher Louisa Moats expressed this position when she alleged that teachers do not want choice. Teachers tell her and other "experts," she claims, "Please don't give us any more choices. Tell us what to do. Give us validated programs that work."[49] Although Moats has repeated this assertion of what teachers tell us, she has yet to offer evidence to substantiate it.

Moats' paper "Whole Language Lives On: The Illusion of 'Balanced' Instruction," published by the right-wing Thomas B. Fordham Foundation and linked in the NICHD reading research division website, contends, as the title implies, that whole language lives but should die. Moats worries that in states where "sound policy" has been established at a statewide level, "whole language may appear to be dying" but because classroom practice has not caught up with policy, "it's not dead at all." Especially harmful is its erroneous conception of "balance," which is not built on the fact that "most children must be taught to read through a structured and protracted process in which they are made aware of sounds and the symbols that represent them, and then learn to apply these skills automatically and attend to meaning." These are Moats' claims, despite the actual findings in the Report's science that neither the superiority of "structured and protracted process" nor the inferiority of whole language teaching has been validated.[50]

Moreover, if one were to select an approach solely on the basis of the Report's own studies, a better choice would be a literature-based/whole language approach because it promotes comprehension right from the start of reading instruction, while not diminishing children's effective use of important strategies and skills. The evidence also suggests that the whole language approach encourages a more positive attitude and enthusiasm toward reading, which in turn might prevent aliteracy, and it is more likely to incorporate extensive writing that promotes learning reading skills, written expression, and vocabulary use.

What Is Omitted? Educational Success Beyond Third Grade

The focus on reading up through the third grade, both in the Report and in the Bush legislation, omits by definition any consideration for the grades beyond third. The focus assumes that once children have attained the basics—or, to use a vocational concept, have gained entry-level knowledge—they will then have the means to ascend higher and higher on the educational ladder. Guiding this assumption is the skills-first adage that children must first learn to read, after which they can read to learn, with the fourth grade usually considered the dividing line between these two steps. This is another theory, not a fact, and is especially suspect because a focus on "ensuring that all children learn to read by third grade" fails to take into account the question of whether, through third grade, children should do work linked to later educational requirements, such as writing, comprehending subject matter ideas and information, reading literature, and reading for sizable periods of time. Within the framework of the two-phase learn to read/read to learn model, the NRP Report and the Bush legislation focus solely on their rendition of the first phase.

The Report's focus on beginning reading is a glaring disregard of the fourth-grade slump.

The omission of any consideration for anything but beginning reading is a glaring disregard of what has been written about the

fourth-grade slump, a point at which children lose interest in reading and cannot cope with new instructional materials and requirements. As Jeanne Chall has observed: "At about grade 4, when the
curriculum requires higher cognitive and linguistic performance,"
many children's reading begins "to slip. They slumped first on word
meanings, particularly on abstract, literary, less common words."
Although Chall was a leading proponent of skills-emphasis, first-
learn-to-read instruction, her recognition of the need for children to
read both widely and in depth, starting in beginning reading, con-
tradicted the educational steps she usually advocated. In her study
of "why poor children fall behind" in reading, for example, Chall
speculated that they did so at fourth grade because they "probably
owned and read fewer books; and they may have been read to less
than middle-class children." Yet, the Report and the Bush legislation
have nothing to say about the issue of how poor children, in their
beginning reading years, are going to duplicate the extensive reading
of middle-class children and thereby reduce the chances of falling
victim to the fourth-grade slump.[51]

Omission of Writing

The entire focus of the Report and the Bush legislation is on reading,
not literacy, and within that focus, writing is minimized, despite the
considerable evidence that writing, especially children's early writing, contributes to learning word skills, expression of ideas, learning
to revise work, and numerous reading activities. The twenty-five-
year perspective of writing researcher Donald Graves is instructive in
this regard:

> In 1978, as part of my Ford Foundation study, I reviewed
> UNESCO funding patterns for literacy programs in various coun-
> tries. Virtually all the literacy programs were geared to helping
> people learn to read. None of them stressed the importance of
> children's ability to write. I find it curious that the great debate in
> America still centers on how to teach our children to read, not on
> their learning to write.[52]

Graves' research has provided extensive understanding of why both
writing and reading must be part of literacy education from the
beginning: "Children who write continually apply phonics, con-

struct syntax, and experience the full range of skills in authoring a text. Writers are more assertive readers and less likely to accept the ideas and texts of others without question since they have been in the reading construction business themselves."[53]

> *For the Report and the Bush legislation, writing is rarely considered.*

His research has contributed to detailed study of children's writing development in kindergarten and first grade. For example, he describes the variety of children's initial writing efforts, such as "using the resources of the letters in their own name" and linking initial letters with a drawing. He advises teachers on the variety of writing they will first encounter in children's initial efforts, such as some children using just one letter, others writing words using the initial and final consonants only, and some having some sight words. He also offers numerous recommendations for reading/writing activities, such as how to help children share their writing in ways that will make them better readers, and how to help those who also read and listen to this writing become better comprehenders.[54]

But for the Report and the Bush legislation, writing is rarely considered. At best, it fleetingly appears as a minor undertaking next to the primary task of reading.

Missing: Ongoing Assessment

Exploration of the question of how teachers can have ongoing knowledge of children's achievements and needs is another essential component of teaching that is absent from the Report. This teacher competence is not simply secondary to the content of reading instruction (phonics, comprehension, etc.); it is fundamental for determining what that content should be. It is fundamental for avoiding a one-size-fits-all pedagogy and for ensuring that a teacher attends to individual differences. This is more than

> *The Report does not explore how teachers can have ongoing knowledge of children's needs in order to address individual differences.*

another void in the Report; it reveals the barrenness of the proposed structured and protracted scripted instructional approach.

An illustration of the ongoing assessment that the Report should have considered is literacy educator Gretchen Owocki's discussion of the "many tools" that provide teachers with knowledge of both what is "necessary in understanding what to teach and how to teach it." One such tool is writing samples (e.g., student-written stories, journals, notes) that reveal "children's knowledge of written language functions, phonics knowledge, spelling development, sense of story, and personal connections to literature." Another is "structured observations of children's" book reading to "track and understand children's early reading development." A third is "oral reading samples" to "understand children's decoding and meaning-making strategies." A fourth is observations of "text retelling," which occurs after silent or oral reading and in which a student draws, writes, acts out, or orally expresses a retelling. Observations of retellings kept over time "show children's progress in learning to make meaning from text."[55]

Regie Routman's work provides numerous research-supported guidelines for observing and evaluating readers. She details procedures for informal reading conferences, note taking as children read, continuous evaluations of student reading that reveal "students' strengths and weaknesses and future teaching directions." She describes evaluations of students who need "to learn and apply phonics" and students who need "to self-monitor for meaning." Evaluations include identifying appropriate books for children to read and learning from students' self-monitoring of their reading. She also explains how to use portfolios of children's work as part of ongoing evaluations.[56]

How can anyone not be critical of a national policy document on "teaching children to read" that does not prominently offer direction to teachers for doing ongoing appraisals of students' literacy progress and for linking instruction to these appraisals? Perhaps this omission was to be expected from a panel that did not include a single beginning reading teacher.

What's Hot?

The omissions in the NRP Report and the mandates enforcing its brand of instruction have contributed to a damaging skewing of reading research and practice. A good indicator of how widespread the damage is can be found in the International Reading Association's poll that asks literacy leaders to identify "hot" and "not hot" topics in reading research and practice for the coming year, as well as those topics that are no longer hot. "Hot" means that the topic is "currently receiving more and positive attention." "Not hot" means that the topic is receiving "less attention or negative attention."

While the majority of respondents (at least 75 percent) listed "balanced reading instruction" as "hot" and "should be hot," it was less so than in the previous year. The decline in attention to "balanced reading instruction" becomes clear when we look at the categories of comprehension, literature-based instruction, word meaning/vocabulary, multicultural literature, portfolio assessment, and whole language, all of which the majority identified as "not hot." Moreover, whole language was deemed not only "not hot" but in deep freeze, with more than 50 percent of the respondents judging it "cold" and a "significant number" of them believing it was cold beyond resuscitation and should, in fact, be removed from the list of topics. Instead, the IRA surveyors decided to keep it because, despite its having become a corpse, "there are still a number of allusions to the term in the popular media." In contrast, the majority of respondents thought phonemic awareness, phonics, and decodable text were "hot" topics.[57] In other words, what is omitted or minimized both in the skills-emphasis model and in the Report appears to have also become omitted or minimized throughout reading education.

> *To receive funds through the Bush legislation, applicants will have to employ skills-emphasis instruction.*

The Shape of the Future?

Despite the lack of scientific evidence supporting it, the NRP model embedded in the Bush legislation is shaping and promises to keep shaping reading education exactly as outlined in the "What's Hot" survey. To receive funds available through the legislation, applicants will have to employ instruction that accords with the legislation's strictures. Evidence for this expectation is in the grant applications for funds through the Reading Excellence Act, the small-sized precursor to the Bush legislation, passed at the end of the Clinton administration, and also requiring scientifically based instruction. I have examined many of these applications and here will describe one from Hawaii that is representative of the instruction that was and will be demanded in order to obtain funds.[58]

The "primary sources" of the "knowledge base" for the "scientifically based reading research" underpinning the Hawaiian grant application include the NRP Report and publications by skills-emphasis educators such as Louisa Moats, Marilyn Adams, Linnea Ehri, Edward Kame'enui, Barbara Foorman, Keith Stanovich, and, of course, Reid Lyon. The research is described as "the rich and robust consensual evidentiary knowledge base," with the term *consensual* meaning, as the application explains, that there is a "broad consensus within the field"—an "auspicious alignment of forces"—agreeing that this kind of education has scientific support. The grant application contains no supportive evidence for these generalities, but presumably the writers of the grant felt these lofty descriptions would be sufficient for those who would read the grant and decide whether to approve it.

The application vividly illustrates what "balanced instruction" really means in the "scientific" model and practice. Instruction in phonological awareness, "the first dimension of beginning reading instruction," is "obligatory, not optional." The second step is "instruction in the alphabetic principle," that is, linking letters and sounds, commonly known as phonics. Comprehension waits patiently while the students work on "fluency with the code," that is, reading smoothly, or, as the proposal describes it, "decoding fluency," because students must first become fluent readers for whom the "decoding processes are automatic, requiring no conscious attention." Fluency precedes comprehension because, the application explains, "if a reader has to spend too much time and energy figuring out what words *are*, she will be unable to concentrate on what the words *mean*." The application does not say that this description is a theory, not a fact, and it certainly does not say that the theory is not supported by the NRP Report's own studies.

If there were any doubt about the emphasis of the beginning reading curriculum that is proposed, one need only look at the description of the teacher training program, which describes the three areas in which teachers will receive "intensive instruction": helping children develop phonemic awareness, "understand the alphabetic principle," and "relate sounds and symbols automatically." And if doubt still remains, one need only look at the instrument to be used to assess this reading education, the Dynamic Indicators of Basic Early Literacy Skills (DIBELS). As the name suggests, it focuses on skills: phonemic awareness, the alphabetic principle, and oral reading fluency—areas described as being aligned with the "big ideas in early reading." Nowhere in the DIBELS evaluation through the third grade is there an assessment of comprehension or writing![59] The other instrument used is the Reading and Curriculum Based Measures, an instrument measuring one-minute oral reading fluency of passages.

Ironically, a study by Hawaiian educator Anna Sumida reveals that this kind of curriculum is exactly *not* what Hawaiian students need most. Sumida found that in a typical classroom profile for second and third graders in a school with primarily poor children, most children (e.g., twenty out of a class of twenty-one) are able to decode at or above grade level; it is their comprehension that lags behind! The data show, Sumida concludes, that "teachers were already doing a fine job teaching phonics skills. It was comprehension that teachers needed to work on, but the programs used in the intervention supported by the REA grant will not address this need!"[60]

> *It is time to demand policy based on an accurate appraisal of what the science actually teaches us.*

Rolling Up Our Sleeves

In several years, if "scientific" reading instruction is allowed to dominate classrooms, and after the educational charade that it is becomes clear, we can be certain that the blame will fall not on national policy or on the scientific reading programs, but on teachers, for not correctly implementing them, and perhaps on the children themselves and their families.

Speaking at a middle school while campaigning for president, Bush asserted, "We want our teachers to be trained so they can meet the obligations, their obligations as teachers. We want them to know how to teach the science of reading. In order to make sure there's not this kind of federal—federal cufflink."[61] By now, everyone is familiar with Bush's verbal foibles and can probably guess what word he had meant to use. Regardless, it unquestionably is time for the parents, educators, politicians, and public who recognize how damaging this "science of reading" is and will be to undo the "cufflink," roll up our sleeves, and demand an end to unjustified mandates and a beginning of a new policy based on an accurate appraisal of what the science actually teaches us.

Endnotes

Chapter 1: The Road to Mandating Instruction and Ending "Wiggle Room"

1. National Reading Panel. 2000. *Report of the National Reading Panel: Teaching Children to Read. Reports of the Subgroups.* Washington, DC: National Institute of Child Health and Human Development; Bush, G. W. 2001. *No Child Left Behind: Legislative Proposal.* Washington, DC: 20 January (www.whitehouse.gov/news/reports/no-child-left-behind.html).

2. *No Child Left Behind Act of 2001* (H.R. 1). 107th Congress. 2002. 8 January (www.thomas.loc.gov).

3. Bush, G. W. 2002. *President Signs Landmark Bill.* 8 January (www .whitehouse.gov/news/releases/2002/01/20020108-1.html).

4. Staples, B. 2002. "How the Clip 'N Snip's Owner Changed Special Education." *New York Times,* 5 January: A10.

5. Coles, G. 2000. *Misreading Reading: The Bad Science That Hurts Children.* Portsmouth, NH: Heinemann.

6. Committee on Education and the Workforce. House of Representatives, U.S. Congress (www.edworkforce.house.gov/hearings.htm).

7. Charlotte Chamber of Commerce. 2001. CMS Partners for School Reform. *What Works in Reading?* 19 January (www.charlottechamber.com).

8. "President Bush's Letter on the Regulation of Carbon Dioxide." 2001. 15 March (www.aip.org/enews/fyi/2001/029.html).

9. Heilprin, J. 2001. "Bush Defends Arsenic Delay, Promises Reduction." *Associated Press Newswires,* 29 March.

10. Bush, G. W. 2001. "Text of a Letter from the President to Senators Hagel, Helms, Craig, and Roberts." 13 March (www.whitehouse.gov /news/releases/2001/03/20010314.html).

11. "President Outlines Education Reform in Boston Speech." 2002. 8 January (www.whitehouse.gov/news/releases/2002/01/20020108-5.html).

12. Bowman, J. L., and D. Harris. 2001. "Paige's Nomination Applauded by Unions, Conservatives Alike." *Education Week*, 10 January: 36; "Profile: Rod Paige." 2000. ABCNEWS.COM. 29 December (www.dailynews.yahoo.com/htx/abc/20001229).

13. Hoyt, J. "Paige Draws Praise from Senate Panel." *Houston Chronicle*, 11 January (www.houstonchronicle.com).

14. Fletcher, M. 2001. "Education Nominee Sails Through His Senate Test." *Washington Post*, 11 January (www.washingtonpost.com).

15. Paige, R. 2001. "Remarks as Prepared for Delivery by U.S. Secretary of Education Rod Paige." *International Reading Association*. New Orleans, LA. 1 May (www.ed.gov/Speeches/05-2001/010501.html).

16. Manzo, K. 1998. "Drilling in Texas." *Education Week*, 10 June (www.educationweek.org).

17. National Reading Panel. 2000. *Report of the National Reading Panel: Teaching Children to Read. Summary Report.* Washington, DC: National Institute of Child Health and Human Development. (Quotations on pp. 7,9.)

18. National Reading Panel. Reports of the Subgroups. (Quotation on p. 2-123.)

19. National Institute of Child Health and Human Development. 2000. "National Reading Panel Reports Combination of Teaching Phonics, Word Sounds, Giving Feedback on Oral Reading Most Effective Way to Teach Reading." Press Release. 13 April (www.nationalreadingpanel.org/Press).

20. Coles, G. 1998. *Reading Lessons: The Debate Over Literacy*. New York: Hill and Wang.

21. Chall, J. 1967. *Learning to Read: The Great Debate*. New York: McGraw-Hill. (Quotation on p. 258.)

22. Goodman, K. S., P. Shannon, Y. S. Freeman, and S. Murphy. 1988. *Report Card on Basal Readers*. Katonah, NY: Richard C. Owen Publishers. (Quotation on p. 63.)

23. Coles. *Reading Lessons*. Ch. 1.

24. Rothman, R. 1990. "From a 'Great Debate' to a Full-Scale War: Dispute Over Teaching Reading Heats Up." *Education Week*, 21 March: 1–11. (Quotation on p. 11.)

25. Coles. *Reading Lessons*. Ch. 1.

26. Goodman, K. 1998. "Comments on the Reading Excellence Act." *Reading Online* (www.readingonline.org).

27. Bennett, W. J. 1986. *First Lessons: A Report on Elementary Education in America*. Washington, DC: U.S. Department of Education.

28. Snow, C., M. S. Burns, and P. Griffin (Eds.). 1998. *Preventing Reading Difficulties in Young Children*. Washington, DC: National Academy Press.

29. Shor, I. 1986. *Culture Wars: School and Society in the Conservative Restoration, 1969–1984*. Boston, MA: Routledge and Kegan Paul. Ch. 3.

30. Altwerger, B., and E. R. Saavedra. 1999. "Foreword." In *Making Justice Our Project: Teachers Working Toward Critical Whole Language Practice*, ed. C. Edelsky, vii–xii. Urbana, IL: National Council of Teachers of English. (Quotations on pp. viii–ix.)

31. Wolfe, P., and L. Poyner. 2001. "Politics and the Pendulum: An Alternative Understanding of the Case of Whole Language as Educational Innovation." *Educational Researcher,* 30: 15–20. (Quotations on p. 18.)

32. Lyon, G. R. 1999. "In Celebration of Science in the Study of Reading Development, Reading Difficulties, and Reading Instruction: The NICHD Perspective." *Issues in Education: Contributions from Educational Psychology,* 5: 85–115. (Quotation on p. 88.)

33. Davis, B. 2001. "Phonics Maven Is at Center of Bush's Education Push." *Wall Street Journal*, 23 April: A24.

34. Bowler, M. 2000. "Eager to Show Schools the Way." *Baltimore Sun*, 6 January (www.sunspot.net).

35. Coles. *Misreading Reading*.

36. Flood, J., and D. Lapp. 2000. "An Interview with Marion Joseph." *The California Reader,* (Fall): 24–39. (Quotations on pp. 37–39.)

37. Pressley, M., and R. Allington. 1999. "Concluding Reflections: What Should Reading Instruction Be the Research Of?" *Issues in Education,* 5: 165–175. (Quotation on p. 169.)

38. Clowes, G. A. 1999. "Reading Is Anything but Natural." *School Reform News* (www.heartland.org/education/jul99/lyon.htm).

39. Moats, L. C. 1990. *Teaching Reading IS Rocket Science: What Expert Teachers of Reading Should Know and Be Able to Do*. Washington, DC: American Federation of Teachers. (Quotations on pp. 5, 10.)

40. Snow et al. *Preventing Reading Difficulties*.

41. National Council of Teachers of English. 1998. "Response to Preventing Reading Difficulties in Young Children." (www.ncte.org/action /nas.htm).

42. Athans, M. 1998. "Report Spells Out Needs on Reading." *Baltimore Sun*, 19 March (www.sunspot.net).

43. Innerst, C. 1998. "Educators Endorse 'Invented Spelling' Also Back Teaching in Native Languages." *Washington Times*, 19 March: A1.

44. National Institute of Child Health and Human Development. 1998. "New Panel to Assess Readiness of Reading Research for Use in Nation's Classrooms." Press Release. 27 March (www.nationalreadingpanel.org /Press/press_rel).

45. National Reading Panel. 1998. "NRP Meeting Archives." Panel Meeting: 24–25 July (www.nationalreadingpanel.org/NRPAbout /Meetings_Archive.htm).

46. National Institute of Child Health and Human Development. 2000. "National Reading Panel Reports Combination of Teaching Phonics, Word Sounds, Giving Feedback on Oral Reading Most Effective Way to Teach Reading." 13 April (www.nichd.nih.gov/new/releases/nrp.htm).

47. Lyon, G. R. 2000. "Statement of Dr. G. Reid Lyon, Education Research and Evaluation and Student Achievement: Quality Counts." Committee on Education and the Workforce, Subcommittee on Early Childhood, Youth and Families. Hearing on: "Options for the Future of the Office of Educational Research and Improvement." 4 May (www.house.gov /ed_workforce/hearings/106th).

48. Henry, T. 2000. "Friends of Phonics Dance for Joy: How Sweet the Sound of Endorsement, Five Decades Later." USA Today, 5 June: D6.

49. Manzo, K. 2000. "Reading Panel Urges Phonics for All in K–6." Education Week, 19 April: 1–14.

50. Bowler, M. 2000. "Phonics Teaching Gets Top Grade." Baltimore Sun, 14 April: 1A.

51. "Teacher Colleges Shun Best Way to Teach Reading." 2000. USA Today, 17 May: 14A.

52. American Federation of Teachers. 2000. "National Reading Panel Report on Research-Based Approaches to Reading Instruction." (www.aft.org/edissues/readpanel.htm).

53. International Reading Association. 2000. "International Reading Association's President Responds to the National Reading Panel Report." 13 April (www.reading.org/advocacy/press000413.html).

54. Hefland, D. 2000. "Report Calls for Multifaceted Reading Strategy." Los Angeles Times, 23 April (www.latimes.com).

55. "Truth About Reading" (Editorial). 2000. Indianapolis Star, 2 May: A27.

56. United States Senate. 2001. "Better Education for Students and Teachers Act: Report of the Committee on Health, Education, Labor, and Pensions to Accompany S.1 Together with Additional Views." Report 107–7. Washington, DC (www.thomas.loc.gov).

57. United States Congress. 2001. "Committee Report to Accompany H.R. 1, Report 107-334." Washington, DC (ftp.loc.gov/pub/thomas/cp107 /hr334.txt).

Chapter 2: "Diversity" of Views

1. National Institute of Child Health and Human Development. 1998. "New Panel to Assess Readiness of Reading Research for Use in Nation's Classrooms." Press Release. 27 March (www.nationalreadingpanel.org /Press/press_rel_3_27_98.htm).

2. Manzo, K. 1998. "NICHD Chief Names Closely Watched Panel on Reading Research." *Education Week*, 8 April (www.edweek.org).

3. Yatvin, J. 2002. "Babes in the Woods: The Wanderings of the National Reading Panel." *Phi Delta Kappan,* 83: 364–369. (Quotations on p. 366.)

4. National Reading Panel. Reports of the Subgroups. (Quotation on p. 1-1.)

5. Yatvin. "Babes in the Woods." (Quotations on pp. 366–367.)

6. National Reading Panel. 1998. "Inaugural Meeting." Meeting Minutes. Bethesda, MD: 24 April (www.nationalreadingpanel.org/NRPAbout /Panel_Meetings/).

7. National Reading Panel. 1998. Meeting Minutes. Bethesda, MD: 24–25 July (www.nationalreadingpanel.org/NRPAbout/Panel_Meetings/).

8. National Reading Panel. Reports of the Subgroups. (Quotation on p. 1-2.)

9. Braunger, J., and J. P. Lewis. 1997. *Building a Knowledge Base in Reading.* Urbana, IL: National Council of Teachers of English.

10. Braunger, J., and J. P. Lewis (Eds.). 1999. *Using the Knowledge Base in Reading.* Newark, DE: International Reading Association.

11. Lewis, J. 1998. "Remarks for National Reading Panel Regional Meeting." Portland, OR. 5 June. I recommend that the reader compare this chapter's excerpts of Lewis' presentation with the summary of the presentation in the Panel's minutes of the meeting and judge the extent to which the latter adequately represents the former. (www.nationalreading panel.org/NRPAbout/Regional_Meetings/portland.htm).

12. National Reading Panel. 1998. Meeting Minutes. Bethesda, MD: 10 September (www.nationalreadingpanel.org/NRPAbout/Panel_Meetings/).

13. National Reading Panel. 1998. Meeting Minutes. Bethesda, MD: 9 November (www.nationalreadingpanel.org/NRPAbout/Panel_Meetings/).

14. Baumann, J. F., J. V. Hoffman, J. Moon, and A. M. Duffy-Hester. 1998. "Where Are Teachers' Voices in the Phonics/Whole Language Debate? Results from a Survey of U.S. Elementary Classroom Teachers." *Reading Teacher,* 51: 636–650.

15. Coles. *Reading Lessons.* 144–147.

16. National Reading Panel. Reports of the Subgroups. (Quotation on p. 1-3.)

Chapter 3: Training and Other Kinds of "Boosts"

1. Lipkin, H. 2001. "Bush's Vision Can Work" (Letter). *Newsday,* 1 July: B7.

2. Garan, E. M. 2002. *Resisting Reading Mandates: How to Triumph with the Truth.* Portsmouth, NH: Heinemann; Krashen, S. 2001. "More Smoke and Mirrors: A Critique of the National Reading Panel Report on Fluency." *Phi Delta Kappan,* October: 119–123; Krashen, S. (in press). "The National Reading Panel Comparison of Whole Language and Phonics: Ignoring the Crucial Variable in Reading." *Talking Points.*

3. Yatvin. "Babes in the Woods." (Quotation on p. 368.)

4. NRP Report. National Reading Panel. Reports of the Subgroups. (Quotations on p. 2-11 to 2-12.)

5. Ehri, L. 1994. "Development of the Ability to Read Words: Update." In *Theoretical Models and Processes of Reading* (4th ed.), eds. R. Ruddell, M. Ruddell, and H. Singer, 323–358. Newark, DE: International Reading Association. (Quotation on p. 325.)

6. Goodman, Y., and K. Goodman. 1994. "To Err Is Human: Learning About Language Processes." In *Theoretical Models and Processes of Reading* (4th ed.), eds. R. Ruddell, M. Ruddell, and H. Singer, 104–123. Newark, DE: International Reading Association. (Quotation on p. 115.)

7. NRP Report. (Quotations on p. 2-36.)

8. Cunningham, A. 1990. "Explicit Versus Implicit Instruction in Phonemic Awareness." *Journal of Experimental Child Psychology,* 50: 429–444. (Quotation on p. 432.)

9. NRP Report. (Quotations on pp. 2-34 to 2-35.)

10. Blachman, B., E. Ball, R. Black, and D. Tangel.1994. "Kindergarten Teachers Develop Phoneme Awareness in Low-Income, Inner-City Classrooms: Does It Make a Difference?" *Reading and Writing: An Interdisciplinary Journal,* 6: 1–18. (Quotation on p. 9, my emphasis.)

11. NRP Report. (Quotation on p. 2-34.)

12. Lie, A. 1991. "Effects of a Training Program for Stimulating Skills in Word Analysis in First-Grade Children." *Reading Research Quarterly,* 26: 234–250. (Quotations on pp. 248–249.)

13. Olofsson, A., and I. Lundberg. 1983. "Can Phonemic Awareness Be Trained in Kindergarten?" *Scandinavian Journal of Psychology,* 24: 35–44. (Quotation on p. 37.)

14. Olofsson and Lundberg. "Can Phonemic Awareness Be Trained?" (Quotation on p. 39.)

15. Olofsson, A., and I. Lundberg. 1985. "Evaluation of Long-Term Effects of Phonemic Awareness Training in Kindergarten: Illustrations of Some Methodological Problems in Evaluation Research." *Scandinavian Journal of Psychology,* 26: 21–34.

16. Haddock, M. 1976. "Effects of an Auditory and an Auditory-Visual Method of Blending Instruction on the Ability of Prereaders to Decode Synthetic Words." *Journal of Educational Psychology,* 68: 825–831. (Quotation on p. 828.)

17. NRP Report. (Quotation on p. 2-36.)

18. Williams, J. 1980. "Teaching Decoding with an Emphasis on Phoneme Analysis and Phoneme Blending." *Journal of Educational Psychology,* 72: 1–15. (Quotation on p. 8.)

19. Ehri, L., and Wilce, L. 1987. "Does Learning to Spell Help Beginners Learn to Read Words?" *Reading Research Quarterly,* 22: 47–65.

20. NRP Report. (Quotation on p. 2-39.)

21. Schneider, W., P. Kuspert, E. Roth, M. Vise, and H. Marx. 1997. "Short- and Long-Term Effects of Training Phonological Awareness in Kindergarten: Evidence from Two German Studies." *Journal of Experimental Child Psychology,* 66: 311–340. (Quotations on pp. 321, 324.)

22. Schneider et al. "Short- and Long-Term Effects." (Quotation on p. 333.)

23. Reitsma, P., and R. Wesseling. 1998. "Effects of Computer-Assisted Training of Blending Skills in Kindergartners." *Scientific Studies of Reading,* 2: 301–320. (Quotation on p. 315.)

24. Brady, S., A. Fowler, B. Stone, and N. Winbury. 1994. "Training Phonological Awareness: A Study with Inner-City Kindergarten Children." *Annals of Dyslexia,* 44: 26–59. (Quotation on p. 30.)

25. Brady et al. "Training Phonological Awareness." (Quotation on p. 44.)

26. O'Connor, R., A. Notari-Syverson, and P. Vadasy. 1996. "Ladders to Literacy: The Effects of Teacher-Led Phonological Activities for

Kindergarten Children with and Without Disabilities." *Exceptional Children,* 63: 117–130. (Quotation on p. 129.)

27. Torgesen, J. K., S. Morgan, and C. Davis. 1992. "Effects of Two Types of Phonological Awareness Training on Word Learning in Kindergarten Children." *Journal of Educational Psychology,* 84: 364–370.

28. Torgesen, J. K., R. K. Wagner, C. A. Roshotte, A. W. Alexander, and T. Conway. 1997. "Preventative and Remedial Interventions for Children with Severe Reading Disabilities." *Learning Disabilities: A Multidisciplinary Journal,* 8: 51–62. (Quotation on p. 57.)

29. Torgesen, J. K., R. K. Wagner, and C. A. Roshotte. 1997. "Prevention and Remediation of Severe Reading Disabilities: Keeping the End in Mind." *Scientific Studies in Reading,* 1: 217–234. (Quotation on p. 220.)

30. NRP Report. (Quotations on pp. 2-40 to 2-41.)

31. NRP Report. (Quotation on p. 2-5.)

Chapter 4: Less Than Impressive Effect Sizes

1. "Starting in 1996, The Diversity Project studied the class of 2000 and amply documented the troubling 'achievement gaps' in Berkeley, where ZIP codes were shown to be reliable predictors of academic achievement." Agony and Amnesia: Why I Voted Against the PCAD Plan. By Shirley Issel, school director (http://parents.berkeley.edu/current/Issel_ltr.html).

2. NRP Report. (Quotations on p. 2-11.)

3. Share, D., A. Jorm, R. Maclean, and R. Matthews. 1984. "Sources of Individual Differences in Reading Acquisition." *Journal of Educational Psychology,* 76: 1309–1324. (Quotation on p. 1313.)

4. NRP Report. (Quotation on p. 2-35.)

5. Brennan, F., and J. Ireson. 1997. "Training Phonological Awareness: A Study to Evaluate the Effects of a Program of Metalinguistic Games in Kindergarten." *Reading and Writing: An Interdisciplinary Journal,* 9: 241–263. (Quotations on pp. 257–258.)

6. NRP Report. (Quotation on p. 2-37.)

7. NRP Report. (Quotation on p. 2-37.)

8. Byrne, B., and R. Fielding-Barnsley. 1991. "Evaluation of a Program to Teach Phonemic Awareness to Young Children." *Journal of Educational Psychology,* 83: 451–455; Byrne, B., and R. Fielding-Barnsley. 1993. "Evaluation of a Program to Teach Phonemic Awareness to Young Children: A 1-Year Follow-Up." *Journal of Educational Psychology,* 85:

104–111; Byrne, B., and R. Fielding-Barnsley. "Evaluation of a Program to Teach Phonemic Awareness to Young Children: A 2- and 3-Year Follow-Up and a New Preschool Trial." *Journal of Educational Psychology*, 87: 488–503.

9. Iversen, S., and W. Tunmer. 1993. "Phonological Processing Skills and the Reading Recovery Program." *Journal of Educational Psychology*, 85: 112–126. (Discussed in Report on p. 2-39.)

10. Tunmer, W., and W. Hoover. 1993. "Phonological Recoding Skill and Beginning Reading." *Reading and Writing: An Interdisciplinary Journal*, 5: 161–179. (Discussed in Report on pp. 2-129 to 2-130.)

11. NRP Report. (Quotation on p. 2-130.)

12. NRP Report. (Quotation on p. 2-40.)

13. Adams, M., B. Foorman, I. Lundberg, and T. Beeler. 1998. *Phonemic Awareness in Young Children: A Classroom Curriculum*. Baltimore, MD: Brookes Publishing Co. (Quotation on p. 2.)

14. Hatcher, P., C. Hulme, and A. Ellis. 1994. "Ameliorating Early Reading Failure by Integrating the Teaching of Reading and Phonological Skills: The Phonological Linkage Hypothesis." *Child Development*, 65: 41–57. (Quotations on pp. 52–53.)

15. NRP Report. (Quotation on p. 2-40.)

16. Ehri, L. C., S. R. Nunes, D. M. Willows, B. V. Schuster, Z. Yaghoub-Zadeh, and T. Shanahan. 2001. "Phonemic Awareness Instruction Helps Children Learn to Read: Evidence from the National Reading Panel's Meta-Analysis." *Reading Research Quarterly*, 36: 250–287. (Quotation on p. 276.)

17. Ehri et al. "Phonemic Awareness Instruction Helps Children." Introducing their evidence, the authors criticized my earlier discussion of the subject, in my book *Misreading Reading*, stating that they "evaluated a greater number of studies." This criticism is factually true but fails to explain the method that I had used to appraise the research on phonemic awareness training. As I explained in *Misreading Reading*, the book was an examination of the studies the researchers associated with the NICHD reading research had themselves identified as evidence of the NICHD claims about the benefits of this training on comprehension. There were other studies I could have reviewed but did not in order to focus only on "their" evidence. Had I introduced additional studies, I would have risked criticism that these additional studies were not ones that the NICHD-related researchers had identified as valuable and, therefore, that my appraisal was far afield and beside the point.

18. Bradley, L., and P. Bryant. 1983. "Categorizing Sounds and Learning to Read: A Causal Connection." *Nature,* 301: 419–421; Bradley, L., and P. Bryant. 1985. *Rhyme and Reason in Reading and Spelling.* Ann Arbor, MI: University of Michigan Press. pp. 75–95.

19. NRP Report. "Appendix F." pp. 279–286.

20. Defior, S., and P. Tudela. 1994. "Effect of Phonological Training on Reading and Writing Acquisition." *Reading and Writing: An Interdisciplinary Journal,* 6: 299–320.

21. Defior and Tudela. "Effect of Phonological Training." (Quotation on p. 303.)

22. Defior and Tudela. "Effect of Phonological Training." (Quotation on p. 316.)

23. Korkman, M., and A. K. Peltomaa. 1993. "Preventive Treatment of Dyslexia by a Preschool Training Program for Children with Language Impairments." *Journal of Clinical Child Psychology,* 22: 277–287. (Quotation on p. 285.)

24. Weiner, S. 1994. "Effects of Phonemic Awareness Training on Low- and Middle-Achieving First Graders' Phonemic Awareness and Reading Ability." *Journal of Reading Behavior,* 26: 277–300. (Quotation on p. 282.)

25. Wise, B., J. King, and R. Olson. 2000. "Individual Differences in Gains from Computer-Assisted Remedial Reading." *Journal of Experimental Child Psychology,* 77: 197–235. (Quotations on pp. 230–231.)

26. Hohn, W., and L. Ehri. 1983. "Do Alphabet Letters Help Prereaders Acquire Phonemic Segmentation Skill?" *Journal of Educational Psychology,* 75: 752–762.

27. O'Connor, R., and J. Jenkins. 1995. "Improving the Generalization of Sound/Symbol Knowledge: Teaching Spelling to Kindergarten Children with Disabilities." *Journal of Special Education,* 29: 255–275. (Quotation on p. 258.)

28. Treiman, R., and J. Baron. 1983. "Phonemic-Analysis Training Helps Children Benefit from Spelling Sound Rules." *Memory and Cognition,* 11: 382–389. (Quotation on p. 382.)

29. Farmer, A., M. Nixon, and R. White. 1976. "Sound Blending and Learning to Read: An Experimental Investigation. *British Journal of Educational Psychology,* 46: 155–163.

30. NRP Report. (Quotation on p. 2-6.)

31. NRP Report. (Quotation on p. 2-4.)

32. Lonigan, C. J., S. R. Burgess, J. L. Anthony, and T. A. Barker. 1998. "Development of Phonological Sensitivity in 2- to 5-Year-Old Children."

Journal of Educational Psychology, 90: 294–311. Also see Coles. *Misreading Reading.* Ch. 9.

33. Coles. *Misreading Reading* and *Reading Lessons.*

34. Ferreiro, E., and A. Teberosky. 1982. *Literacy Before Schooling.* Portsmouth, NH: Heinemann.

Chapter 5: Systematic Phonics Beats Whole Language!

1. NRP Report. (Quotations on p. 2-134.)

2. Wilson, K., and C. Norman. 1998. "Differences in Word Recognition Based on Approach to Reading Instruction." *Alberta Journal of Educational Research,* 44: 221–230. (Quotation on p. 229.)

3. Wilson and Norman. "Differences in Word Recognition." (Quotation on p. 228.)

4. Klesius, J., P. Griffith, and P. Zielonka. 1991. "A Whole Language and Traditional Instruction Comparison: Overall Effectiveness and Development of the Alphabetic Principle." *Reading Research and Instruction,* 30: 47–61. (Quotations on p. 59.)

5. Griffith, P., J. Klesius, and J. Kromey. 1992. "The Effect of Phonemic Awareness on the Literacy Development of First Grade Children in a Traditional or a Whole Language Classroom." *Journal of Research in Childhood Education,* 6: 85–92. (Quotation on p. 87.)

6. Griffith et al. "The Effect of Phonemic Awareness." (Quotations on p. 90.)

7. Griffith et al. "The Effect of Phonemic Awareness." (Quotations on p. 91.)

8. Foorman, B., D. Francis, J. Fletcher, C. Schatschneider, and P. Mehta. 1998. "The Role of Instruction in Learning to Read: Preventing Reading Failure in At-Risk Children." *Journal of Educational Psychology,* 90: 37–55.

9. Coles. *Misreading Reading.* See Ch. 3 on the "Foorman study."

10. www.sra-4kids.com.

11. Eldredge, L. 1991. "An Experiment with a Modified Whole Language Approach in First-Grade Classrooms." *Reading Research and Instruction,* 30: 21–38. (Quotation on p. 35.)

12. Eldredge. "An Experiment." (Quotation on p. 26.)

13. Eldredge. "An Experiment." (Quotation on p. 33.)

14. Eldredge. "An Experiment." (Quotation on p. 31.)

15. Evans, M., and T. Carr. 1985. "Cognitive Abilities, Conditions of Learning, and the Early Development of Reading Skill." *Reading Research Quarterly*, 20: 327–350. (Quotation on p. 331. My emphasis.)

16. Santa, C., and T. Hoien. 1999. "An Assessment of Early Steps: A Program for Early Intervention of Reading Problems." *Reading Research Quarterly*, 34: 54–79. (Quotation on p. 58.)

17. NRP Report. (Quotations on p. 2-173.)

18. Santa and Hoien. "An Assessment of Early Steps." (Quotations on p. 67.)

19. Santa and Hoien. "An Assessment of Early Steps." (Quotation on p. 70.)

20. NRP Report. "Appendix G." p. 2-175.

21. Freppon, P. 1991. "Children's Concepts of the Nature and Purpose of Reading in Different Instructional Settings." *Journal of Reading Behavior*, 23: 139–163. (Quotation on p. 159.)

22. For example: Goodman, Y. M. (Ed.). 1990. *How Children Construct Literacy*. Newark, DE: International Reading Association.

23. Freppon. "Children's Concepts." (Quotation on p. 139.)

24. Freppon. "Children's Concepts." (Quotation on p. 144.)

25. Freppon. "Children's Concepts." (Quotations on p. 152.)

26. Freppon. "Children's Concepts." (Quotations on p. 153.)

27. Freppon. "Children's Concepts." (Quotations on p. 152.)

28. For example: LeBerge, D., and S. J. Samuels. 1985. "Toward a Theory of Automatic Information Processing in Reading." In *Theoretical Models and Processes of Reading*, eds. Harry Singer and Robert Ruddell, 689–718. Newark, DE: International Reading Association.

29. Traweek, K., and V. Berninger. 1997. "Comparisons of Beginning Literacy Programs: Alternative Paths to the Same Learning Outcome." *Learning Disability Quarterly*, 20: 160–168.

30. Stuart, M. 1999. "Getting Ready for Reading: Early Phoneme Awareness and Phonics Teaching Improves Reading and Spelling in Inner-City Second Language Learners." *British Journal of Educational Psychology*, 69: 587–605. (Quotation on p. 590.)

31. NRP Report. (Quotations on p. 2-134.)

Chapter 6: "These [Phonics] Facts Should Persuade Educators and the Public"

1. NRP Report. (Quotations on pp. 2-132 to 2-135.)

2. Oakland, T., J. Black, G. Stanford, N. Nussbaum, and R. Balise. 1998. "An Evaluation of the Dyslexia Training Program: A Multisensory Method for Promoting Reading in Students with Reading Disabilities." *Journal of Learning Disabilities,* 31: 140–147. (Quotation on p. 143.)

3. Oakland et al. "An Evaluation." (Quotaton on p. 146.)

4. Lovett, M., M. Ransby, N. Hardwick, M. Johns, and S. Donaldson. 1989. "Can Dyslexia Be Treated? Treatment-Specific and Generalized Treatment Effects in Dyslexic Children's Reponse to Remediation." *Brain and Language,* 37: 90–121. (Quotations on p. 96.)

5. Lovett et al. "Can Dyslexia Be Treated?" (Quotation on p. 112.)

6. Lovett, M., P. Warren-Chaplin, M. Ransby, and S. Borden. 1990. "Training the Word Recognition Skills of Reading Disabled Children: Treatment and Transfer Effects." *Journal of Educational Psychology,* 82: 769–780. (Quotation on p. 777.)

7. Lovett, M., and K. Steinbach. 1997. "The Effectiveness of Remedial Programs for Reading Disabled Children of Different Ages: Does the Benefit Decrease for Older Children?" *Learning Disability Quarterly,* 20: 189–210; Lovett, M., L. Lacerenza, S. Borden, J. Frijters, K. Steinbach, and M. DePalma. 2000. "Components of Effective Remediation for Developmental Reading Disabilities: Combining Phonological and Strategy-Based Instruction to Improve Outcomes." *Journal of Educational Psychology,* 92: 263–283.

8. Lovett et al. "Components of Effective Remediation." (Quotation on p. 267.)

9. Lovett et al. "Components of Effective Remediation." (Quotation on p. 268.)

10. NRP Report. (Quotation on p. 2-131.)

11. Lovett et al. "Components of Effective Remediation." (Quotation on p. 279.)

12. NRP Report. (Quotation on p. 2-137.)

13. Torgesen, J., R. Wagner, C. Rashotte, E. Rose, P. Lindamood, T. Conway, and C. Garvan. 1999. "Preventing Reading Failure in Young Children with Phonological Processing Disabilities: Group and Individual Responses to Instruction." *Journal of Educational Psychology,* 91: 579–593. (Quotation on p. 582.)

14. Torgesen et al. "Preventing Reading Failure." (Quotation on p. 583.)

15. NRP Report. (Quotations on p. 2-128.)

16. Torgesen et al. "Preventing Reading Failure." (Quotation on p. 589.)

17. Torgesen et al. "Preventing Reading Failure." (Quotations on p. 590.)

18. Brown, I., and R. Felton. 1990. "Effects of Instruction on Beginning Reading Skills in Children at Risk for Reading Disability." *Reading and Writing: An Interdisiplinary Journal,* 2: 223–241. (Quotation on p. 223.)

19. NRP Report. "Appendix G." p. 2-169.

20. Goodman, K. S., P. Shannon, Y. S. Freeman, and S. Murphy. 1988. *Report Card on Basal Readers.* Katonah, NY: Richard C. Owen Publishers. (Quotations on p. 72.)

21. NRP Report. (Quotation on p. 2-137.)

22. Blachman, B., D. Tangel, E. Ball, R. Black, and D. McGraw. 1999. "Developing Phonological Awareness and Word Recognition Skills: A Two-Year Intervention with Low-Income, Inner-City Children." *Reading and Writing: An Interdisiplinary Journal,* 11: 239–273. (Quotations on p. 239.)

23. Blachman et al. "Developing Phonological Awareness." (Quotation on p. 268.)

24. NRP Report. (Quotation on p. 2-133.)

25. Mantzicopoulos P., D. Morrison, E. Stone, and W. Setrakian. 1992. "Use of the SEARCH/TEACH Tutoring Approach with Middle-Class Students at Risk for Reading Failure." *Elementary School Journal,* 92: 573–586. (Quotations on p. 583. My emphasis.)

26. Marston, D., S. Deno, K Dongil, K. Diment, and D. Rogers. 1995. "Comparison of Reading Intervention Approaches for Students with Mild Disabilities." *Exceptional Children,* 62: 20–37. (Quotations on pp. 34–36.)

27. Gersten, R., C. Darch, and M. Gleason. 1988. "Effectiveness of a Direct Instruction Academic Kindergarten for Low-Income Students." *Elementary School Journal,* 89: 227–240. (Quotation on p. 231.)

28. Gersten et al. "Effectiveness of a Direct Instruction." (Quotation on p. 235.)

29. Archer, J. 1997. "Strike Ends, Struggles Continue for Illinois District." *Education Week,* 15 October (www.edweek.org).

30. Kozol, J. 1991. *Savage Inequalities.* New York: Crown Publishers. (Quotations on pp. 7–38.)

31. Peterson, M., and L. Haines. 1992. "Orthographic Analogy Training with Kindergarten Children: Effects on Analogy Use, Phonemic

Segmentation, and Letter-Sound Knowledge." *Journal of Reading Behavior,* 24: 109–127. (Quotation on p. 123.)

32. Peterson and Haines. "Orthographic Analogy Training." (Quotations on p. 124. My emphasis.)

33. NRP Report. (Quotation on p. 2-132.)

Chapter 7: Encouraging Students to Read More

1. NRP Report. (Quotations on p. 3-21.)

2. NRP Report. (Quotations on p. 3-21.)

3. NRP Report. (Quotations on p. 3-28.)

4. Burley, J. E. 1980. "Short-Term, High Intensity Reading Practice Methods for Upward Bound Students: An Appraisal." *Negro Educational Review,* 31: 156–161. (Quotation on p. 156.)

5. Burley. "Short-Term." (Quotation on pp. 160–161.)

6. NRP Report. (Quotations on p. 3-25.)

7. Shanahan, T. 2000. "Reading Panel: A Member Responds to a Critic" (Letter). *Education Week,* 31 May: 38 (www.edweek.org).

8. Burley. "Short-Term." (Quotation on p. 158.)

9. Shanahan. "Reading Panel."

10. Burley. "Short-Term." (Quotation on p. 158.)

11. NRP Report. (Quotation on p. 3-25.)

12. Cline, R., and G. Kretke. 1980. "An Evaluation of Long-Term SSR in the Junior High School." *Journal of Reading,* 23: 503–506. (Quotation on p. 503.)

13. Cline and Kretke. "An Evaluation." (Quotations on pp. 505–506.)

14. NRP Report. (Quotation on p. 3-24.)

15. Collins, C. 1980. "Sustained Silent Reading Periods: Effects on Teachers' Behaviors and Students' Achievement." *Elementary School Journal,* 81: 108–114. (Quotation on p. 111.)

16. Collins. "Sustained Silent Reading." (Quotation p. 112.)

17. Davis, Z. T. 1988. "A Comparison of the Effectiveness of Sustained Silent Reading and Directed Reading Activity on Students' Reading Achievement." *High School Journal,* 72 (1): 46–48. (Quotation on p. 47.)

18. NRP Report. (Quotations on p. 3-25.)

19. Shanahan. "Reading Panel."

20. Holt, S. B., and F. S. O'Tuel. 1989. "The Effect of Sustained Silent Reading and Writing on Achievement and Attitudes of Seventh and Eighth Grade Students Reading Two Years Below Grade Level." *Reading Improvement,* 26: 290–297. (Quotation on p. 296.)

21. Langford, J. C., and E. G. Allen. 1983. "The Effects of U.S.S.R. on Students' Attitudes and Achievement." *Reading Horizons,* 23: 194–200. (Quotation on p. 196.)

22. NRP Report. (Quotation on p. 3-24.)

23. Krashen, S. 2001. "More Smoke and Mirrors." (Quotation on p. 120.)

24. Shanahan. "Reading Panel."

25. NRP Report. (Quotation on p. 3-26.)

26. Manning, G., and M. Manning. 1984. "What Models of Recreational Reading Make a Difference?" *Reading World,* 23: 375–380. (Quotation on p. 379.)

27. NRP Report. (Quotation on p. 3-26.)

28. Morrow, L. M., and C. S. Weinstein. 1986. "Encouraging Voluntary Reading: The Impact of a Literature Program on Children's Use of Library Centers." *Reading Research Quarterly,* 21: 330–346. (Quotations on pp. 330, 342.)

29. Peak, J., and M. W. Dewalt. 1994. "Reading Achievement: Effects of Computerized Reading Management and Enrichment." *ERS Spectrum,* 12(1): 31–34.

30. NRP Report. (Quotations on p. 3-26.)

31. Reutzel, D. R., and Hollingsworth, P. M. 1991. "Reading Comprehension Skills: Testing the Distinctiveness Hypothesis." *Reading Research and Instruction,* 30: 32–46.

32. Reutzel and Hollingsworth. "Reading Comprehension Skills." (Quotations on pp. 41, 43.)

33. Vollands, S. R., K. Topping, and R. M. Evans. 1999. "Computerized Self-Assessment of Reading Comprehension with the Accelerated Reader: Action Research." *Reading and Writing Quarterly,* 15: 197–211. (Quotation on p. 204.)

34. NRP Report. (Quotation on p. 3-26.)

35. Vollands et al. "Computerized Self-Assessment." (Quotation on p. 207.)

36. NRP Report. (Quotation on p. 3-26.)

37. NRP Report. (Quotation on p. 3-28.)

38. Strauss, V. 2002. "Relying on Science in Teaching Kids to Read." *Washington Post,* 26 February: A11.

39. Allington, R. L. 2001. *What Really Matters for Struggling Readers: Designing Research-Based Programs.* New York: Longman. (Quotations on pp. 25, 33.)

40. NRP Report. (Quotation on p. 3-21.)

41. Weeks, L. 2001. "The No-Book Report, Skim It and Weep: More and More Americans Who Can Read Are Choosing Not To. Can We Afford to Write Them Off?" *Washington Post,* 14 May: C1.

42. Morrow and Weinstein. "Encouraging Voluntary Reading." (Quotations on pp. 331, 332, 344.)

43. Taberski, S. 2000. *On Solid Ground: Strategies for Teaching Reading K–3.* Portsmouth, NH: Heinemann. (Quotation on p. 7.)

44. Keene, E. O., and S. Zimmerman. 1997. *Mosaic of Thought: Teaching Comprehension in a Reader's Workshop.* Portsmouth, NH: Heinemann. (Quotation on p. 34.)

45. Keene and Zimmerman. *Mosaic of Thought.* (Quotation on p. 82.)

46. Keene and Zimmerman. *Mosaic of Thought.* (Quotation on p. 82.)

47. Keene and Zimmerman. *Mosaic of Thought.* (Quotation on p. 40.)

48. Taberski. *On Solid Ground.* (Quotations on pp. 95, 172.)

49. American Federation of Teachers. 2000. "Panel Cites Effective Reading Strategies." 23 May (www.aft.org/edisssues/readpanel.htm).

50. Manzo. "Reading Panel Urges Phonics for All."

Chapter 8: Unhandcuffing Reading Education

1. Shaywitz, S., and B. Shaywitz. 2001. "Bringing Science to the Teaching of Reading, Comment on the *Wall Street Journal* Profile of Reid Lyon." Council for Basic Education, 2 May (www.c-b-e.org/makediff/qlyon.htm).

2. "Governor Bush Highlights Reading in Virginia." 1999. Press Release, 22 May (www.georgebush.com).

3. Bush, L. 1999. "Reading: The Key to Success." *Moore County News-Press,* 9 September (www.moorenews.com).

4. Schemo, D. 2001. "Easy Approval Seen for Education Official." *New York Times,* 11 January: A21.

5. McGraw-Hill. 2001. "The Harold W. McGraw Jr. Prize in Education: Past Winners." (http://www.mcgraw-hill.com/community/mcgraw_prize /2001/past.html).

6. Lacey, M. 2001. "Education Dept. Will Get Biggest Budget Increase, Bush Says." *New York Times*, 22 February: A13.

7. Haney, W. 2000. "The Myth of the Texas Miracle in Education: Pt. 7: Other Evidence." *Education Policy Analysis Archives*, 19 August: (epaa.asu.edu/epaa/v8n41). (Quotation on p. 28.)

8. Haney. "The Myth of the Texas Miracle. Pt. 7."

9. Haney. "The Myth of the Texas Miracle: Pt. 6: Educators' Views of the TAAS." (Quotation on p. 2.)

10. Schrag, P. "Too Good to Be True." *The American Prospect*, 3 January (www.prospect.org).

11. Morse, J. 2000. "Does Texas Make the Grade?" *CNN News*, 4 September (www.cnn.com/ALLPOLITICS/time/2000/09/11/texas.html).

12. McNeil, L., and A. Valenzuela. 1998. "The Harmful Impact of the TAAS System of Testing in Texas: Beneath the Accountability Rhetoric." *The Civil Rights Project*. Harvard University (www.law.Harvard.edu /civilrights).

13. Klein, S. P., L. S. Hamilton, D. F. McCaffrey, and B. M. Stecher. 2000. "What Do Test Scores in Texas Tell Us?" October. *RAND Education* (www.rand.org/publications/IP/IP202/).

14. Mintz, John. 2000. "Report Questions Bush on Education." *Washington Post*, 24 October (www.washingtonpost.com).

15. Haney. "The Myth of the Texas Miracle: Pt. 7."

16. Balfanz, R., and N. Legters. 2001. "How Many Central City High Schools Have a Severe Dropout Problem, Where Are They Located, and Who Attends Them? Initial Estimates Using the Common Core of Data." January. *The Civil Rights Project*. Harvard University (www.law.Harvard .edu/groups/civilrights).

17. Texans for Public Justice. 2000. "State of the Lone Star State: How Life in Texas Measures Up, Education" (http://www.tpj.org/reports/sos/).

18. Koenig, S. 2000. "Bush's Report Card Shows Progress." *Primary Monitor*, 23 January (www.primarymonitor.com); Maxey, G. 2000. "Lies Can't Mask Bush's Bad Record on Texas Kids." *Houston Chronicle*, 31 July (www.houstonchronicle.com).

19. Begala, P. 2000. *Is Our Children Learning? The Case Against George W. Bush*. New York: Simon and Schuster. (Quotation on pp. 35–36.)

20. Texas Educational Agency. 2000. *A Report to the 77 Texas Legislature* (www.tea.state.tx.us/ESC/support/77rd.pdf).

21. Ivins, M. 2001. "Texas Legislature Busy Reversing Course from Bush Era." *Contra Costa Times*, 10 April (www.contracostatimes.com).

22. Maxey. "Lies Can't Mask."

23. Texans for Public Justice. "State of the Lone Star State, Human Services."

24. Texans for Public Justice. "State of the Lone Star State." (Quotation on p. 62.)

25. Robelen, E. W. 2001. "Bush Unveils Outline for Education Spending." *Education Week*, 7 March: 1–30.

26. Department of Education. 2002. *Department of Education Fiscal Year 2002 Congressional Action*. 23 January (www.ed.gov/offices/OUS/Budget02 /02app.pdf); Mohammed, A. 2002 "Bush Plans Largest Military Budget Increase in 20 Years." Reuters News, 24 January.

27. Ornstein, C. 2001. "Library Group Throws Book at Bush Over Proposed Cuts." *Dallas Morning News*, 13 April (www.dallasnews.com).

28. National Writing Project. "NWP Legislative Updates" (www .writingproject.org/Resources/dc.htm).

29. Trotter, A., and D. J. Hoff. 2002. "Technology Programs in and out of Education Department Take Big Hit in Budget." *Education Week*, 13 February: 33.

30. Butler, A., and M. Gish. 2002. *Head Start: Background and Funding.* CRS Report for Congress. Washington, DC: Congressional Research Service, Library of Congress. 6 February.

31. Trotter and Hoff. "Technology Programs."

32. Edelman, M. W. 2001. "Statement for the Record of the Children's Defense Fund Before the House Budget Committee," 1 August. Washington, DC: United States House of Representatives (http://www .house.gov/budget_democrats/hearings.htm); National Center for Children in Poverty. 2002. *Child Poverty Fact Sheet: Low-Income Children in the United States: A Brief Demographic Profile* (www.cpmcnet .columbia.edu/dept/nccp/ycpf.html).

33. Edelman. "Statement for the Record."

34. Begala. *Is Our Children Learning?* (Quotation on p. 34.)

35. Huffington, A. 2001. "Uncurious George." 23 August (www .ariannaonline.com/columns/files/082301.html).

36. Fairbank, K. 1999. "Bush Says Media Have Treated Him Fairly After All." Associated Press (www.texnews.com/abilene2000/elec/bush0827 .html).

37. Tawa, R. 2001. "There'll Be No Bard at the Inauguration." *Los Angeles Times*, 11 January (www.latimes.com/news/politics/decision2000 /inauguration/lat_poet010111.htm).

38. Miller, M. C. 2001. *The Bush Dyslexicon: Observations of a National Disorder*. New York: Norton. (Quotation on p. 131.)

39. Miller. *The Bush Dyslexicon*. (Quotation on p. 129.)

40. Miller. *The Bush Dyslexicon*. (Quotations on p. 130.)

41. Huffington. "Uncurious George."

42. Bush, L. 2002. "Remarks by Mrs. Bush, House Education and Workforce Committee." Washington, DC: United States House of Representatives, 14 March (www.whitehouse.gov/firstlady).

43. Lyon, G. R. 1999. "Statement of G. Reid Lyon, House Committee on Education and Workforce." Washington, DC: United States House of Representative, 27 July (www.edworkforce.house.gov/hearings/106th/fc /esea72799/lyon.htm).

44. Northup, A. 2001. "Testimony of Anne Northup: No Child Left Behind." House Committee on Education and the Workforce. Washington, DC: United States House of Representative, 28 March (www.edworkforce.house.gov/hearings/107th/fc/members32801 /northup.htm).

45. Shaywitz and Shaywitz. "Bringing Science to the Teaching of Reading."

46. NRP Report. (Quotations on pp. 2-28, 2-40, 2-41.)

47. NRP Report. (Quotation on p. 2-92.)

48. NRP Report. (Quotation on p. 2-134.)

49. Rossi, R. 2001. "Reading Panel Turns the Page." *Chicago Sun Times*, 6 April (www.nrrf.org/news_CST_4-6-01.htm).

50. Moats, L. C. 2000. "Whole Language Lives On: The Illusion of 'Balanced' Instruction." Thomas B. Fordham Foundation (www .edexcellence.net/library/wholelang/moats.html).

51. Chall, J. S., V. A. Jacobs, and L. E. Baldwin. 1990. *The Reading Crisis: Why Poor Children Fall Behind*. Cambridge, MA: Harvard University Press. (Quotations on pp. 52–53.)

52. Graves, D. 1994. *A Fresh Look at Writing*. Portsmouth, NH: Heinemann. (Quotation on pp. 44–45.)

53. Graves, D. 2001. Personal Communication.

54. Graves. *A Fresh Look*. (Quotation on p. 145.)

55. Owocki, G. 2001. *Make Way for Literacy!: Teaching the Way Young Children Learn*. Portsmouth, NH: Heinemann. (Quotations on pp. 23–31.)

56. Routman, R. 2000. *Conversations: Strategies for Teaching, Learning, and Evaluating*. Portsmouth, NH: Heinemann. (Quotations on pp. 113, 118–119.)

57. Cassidy, J., and D. Cassidy. 2002. "What's Hot, What's Not for 2002." *Reading Today*, December 2001/January 2002 (www.reading.org /publications/rty/archives/whats_hot.html).

58. Hawaii Department of Education. 2001. *State of Hawaii "Reading First" Initiative: Building, Implementing, and Sustaining a Statewide Scientifically-Based Beginning Reading Model*. Reading Excellence Act Grant Application.

59. "The Dynamic Indicators of Basic Early Literacy Skills (DIBELS)" (www.dibels.uoregon.edu).

60. Sumida, A. 2001. "IRI Informal Reading Inventory Analysis of Decoding and Comprehension Levels in Hawaiian Children." National Council of Teachers of English Conference, Baltimore, MD.

61. Bush, G. W. 2000. (At Fritsche Middle School, Milwaukee, 30 March). In *The Complete Bushisms*, eds. J. Weisberg and B. Curtis. (www.slate.msn .com/?id=76886).

Appendix

Chapter Two: "Diversity" of Views

Additional replies from teachers:

Lalia Kirk: "I do recognize that my students need a degree of phonological awareness as *one* strategy when they read. What I object to is presenting that as the *only* strategy they need. There is a variety of good strategies that help children as they encounter unfamiliar words—using meaning, guess and check, looking at the beginning sound, looking for familiar chunks in the word, skip and go back, and so forth. Why would you limit the children to one strategy when they need *all* of them to be fluent readers?

"If I spent most of my time on phonics and phonological awareness, it would make my students think that 'sounding out' is the only, or at least the most important, strategy. Down that road would be a bunch of strategy-dependent readers—children who *only* knew how to sound out words at the expense of the other strategies. There's an old saying, 'If all you have is a hammer, the whole world looks like a nail.'"

K. K. Hudson-Bates: "Skills are key in learning to read. Indeed, I include daily work on them. But to say that they are the main ingredients to helping children learn to read is to miss the point. I think that a *desire*, indeed, a *need* to read is probably the most important factor and therefore that is what I am constantly working on— through fun books available to students, a readers' theater performance, notes from me to them, treasure hunts, journal writing, bookmaking, and so on. The 'skills' part of the teaching is the easier part; finding ways to create a need to read/write is what takes creativity. That, at least, is where I've needed to put all my energies as I learn to teach first graders."

Tanya Sharon: "I think skills are very important in learning to read but I don't think they can be taught without other things in place. Most of the children I teach do not have access to good children's literature outside of my classroom. Some may be motivated to succeed with the drills in skills because they want to do well in school, to please the teacher, to please their parents, or to earn money or other incentives. But without the opportunity to know good literature or to explore informational books that are of interest to them, they don't develop an intrinsic motivation. Children should not think of reading as a set of skills rather than an interaction with the author or with the ideas presented on the page.

"The skills are best taught in the context of good literature. When the children encounter a difficult passage in an interesting book and the teacher has been able to show them then and there a new skill that 'unlocks' it for them, they feel that 'aha' moment. They continue to feel that excitement as they use that skill in the next few days, reading books they want to read and telling their friends and family how they can figure out the 'hard' words. Motivated by their own joy in the experience of reading, they will continue to practice that skill even when there is no 'assignment.' And, because reading is always more than an isolated skill, is always about making meaning from what is on the page, they will think about what they read in a much different way than if they were reading to fill out a worksheet or answer a question on a test."

Alice Pickel: "I do ongoing evaluations in order to plan for instruction that would be useful for any given student at any given time. There is no skill that one can name that would be useful for all the children at the same time or that all children need to learn at the same time. I believe that when a particular skill is needed, it usually takes very little instructional time to help the child past that point. I listen to my students reading in order to know what their stumbling blocks are and teach directly those particular skills."

Shelley Hartman: "Most of the [skills-emphasis researchers] aren't in the 'trenches' so to speak; they are not in the classroom. I have spent my whole career (seventeen years) researching how to teach reading in the midst of real subjects, the children. I have come to understand that reading is more than isolated skills, phonological awareness, and fluency. [Learning to read should not be seen] as a linear, sequential set of skills. Learning to read is a process that one goes through in an individually meaningful way. It is the teacher's job to figure out what that is. I did not specifically talk about skills in my reply—not because I don't think skills are important, but because there is so much more to look at in the process of reading. There is no one set way to teach every child. Access to a variety of books that can be appropriate for a variety of interests and developmental levels is also what ensures that children become lifelong lovers of reading."

Chapter 3: Training and Other Kinds of "Boosts"

Warrick et al. (1993)

The study used PA training with a group of "language-delayed kindergarten children" and compared them with a group of similar children who did not use the training program and a group of normally developing children. A year after the training program, the training group's scores on measures of "real-word reading" and "nonword reading" were significantly superior to those of the language-delayed control group and were approximately at the same levels with the normally developing children.

What kind of instruction did the comparison groups receive? Researchers Nicola Warrick and her colleagues explained that the control groups were "in various classroom environments within the same school system" but gave no information about the kind of reading instruction used in these classrooms.

Therefore, although we are again left agreeing that skills are important in beginning reading, we are also given no idea about how they were taught—or if they were taught—in these "various classroom environments." We have no idea what kind of classroom instruction the training program boosted. For a national report on reading, this study offers no direction for the kind of instruction teachers should employ. And once more we have a study whose outcome measure and definition of reading do not go beyond the word level. (Warrick, N., H. Rubin, and S. Rowe-Walsh. 1993. "Phoneme Awareness in Language-Delayed Children: Comparative Studies and Intervention." *Annals of Dyslexia,* 43: 153–173. Quotations on p. 168.)

Korkman and Peltomaa (1993)

This study was based on trying to remedy deficient regular reading education with an early skills-training program. Specifically, a group of Finnish kindergartners, identified as having "language impairments, suggesting a risk of later reading and spelling disorders," were put in a PA training program and were compared with a control group that engaged in no written language activities because in Finland "formal reading and spelling instruction starts the year the child reaches seven years of age." At the end of first grade, predictably, the children who had received two years of written language work had higher scores on reading and writing tests.

Can anything from this study apply to national reading policy? We could conclude that it is sound to have young children who are likely to have reading and spelling problems engage in written language activities in kindergarten. Can we conclude that a phonemic training program is necessary for children who might have trouble learning to read? No, because the Finnish beginning reading program, the researchers explained, is "taught very rapidly" but seems to be most successful for "normal children," who "toward the end of the year" usually "master reading texts and writing on a sentence level." Given this outcome, the most important conclusion to draw is that the Finnish beginning reading instruction should change because of its limited effectiveness. There is nothing useful for U.S. national reading policy in an adjunct program that helps buttress inadequate regular reading education. (Korkman, M., and A. Peltomaa. 1993. "Preventive Treatment of Dyslexia by a Preschool Training Program for Children with Language Impairments." *Journal of Clinical Child Psychology,* 22: 277–287. Quotations on pp. 279, 285.)

Lundberg et al. (1988)

The "compared with what?" problem was also apparent in a study that had the control group follow "the regular preschool program, which in Denmark emphasizes social and aesthetic aspects of development and rather deliberately avoids formal cognitive and linguistic training, including early reading instruction." This group was compared with another that received phonemic awareness training for almost the entire year. When Danish research Ingvar Lundberg and his colleagues tested the groups at the end of grades 1 and 2, after the training group had had an extra year of reading-related instruction, the differences in achievement between the groups were what one would expect. We could conclude that Danish kindergarten should implement written language activities because there are none, but the study offers no evidence for the effectiveness of phonemic awareness training over other literacy-related approaches in kindergarten. (Lundberg, I., J. Frost, and O. Petersen. 1988. "Effects of an Extensive Program for Stimulating Phonological Awareness in Preschool Children." *Reading Research Quarterly*, 23: 263–284. Quotation on p. 268.)

Davidson and Jenkins (1994)

The Report states that Marcia Davidson and Joseph Jenkins gave "kindergartners with low PA one of four possible types of training"— segmentation alone, blending alone, and segmentation and blending combined—and found that "on measures of reading and spelling, both the segmentation and combination groups performed similarly and outperformed the control group." And what were the control group children doing while the experimental groups were practicing separating and/or combining sounds in words? They were listening to stories, doing some exercises in letter formation, and learning the names and sounds of letters. They were not doing any kind of beginning written language activities that might have contributed to their performance on tests of learning to read and spell words.

Moreover, the Report does not explain that this short-term study, lasting between eight and twelve weeks, depending on the rate children learned, found very limited transference of PA training to word reading and spelling. As the researchers explained, "phonemic generalization test" results "indicated that children tended to acquire the particular generalizations they were taught but performed poorly on uninstructed generalizations." (Davidson, M., and J. Jenkins. 1994. "Effects of Phonemic Processes on Word Reading and Spelling." *Journal of Educational Research*, 87: 148–157. Quotation for the NRP Report on p. 2-38. Quotation for Davidson and Jenkins on p. 148.)

Castle et al. (1994)

A study that included whole language teaching found, according to the Report, that "adding PA instruction to a whole language program enhances students' decoding and spelling skills but not their other reading skills": The phonemic awareness "trained group spelled more words and decoded many more pseudowords than the two control groups." However, the Report continues, "the groups did not differ in reading real words or in reading connected text." In other words, phonemic awareness did not achieve all the written language benefits anticipated, but whole language teaching was improved when phonemic training was added to it.

The Report does not make clear that the aim of the researchers, Jillian Castle and colleagues, was "to determine whether the addition of phonemic awareness training had a greater effect on learning to spell than did the regular writing program alone," one in which "children are encouraged to write their own stories and to invent their own spelling."

The spelling results the Report describes were obtained in a pseudoword spelling test and a formal spelling test. The Report omits the results of spelling tests that evaluated the students' ability to spell in dictated sentences, to generate and write words they knew, and to identify letters. For these tests—measures closer to the creation and spelling of actual, complex written language—there were no group differences.

This is another study in which students in a program described as whole language attained achievement levels comparable to those in skills training, showing the whole language program was at least as effective. (Castle, J., J. Riach, and T. Nicholson. 1994. "Getting Off to a Better Start in Reading and Spelling: The Effects of Phonemic Awareness Instruction Within a Whole Language Program." *Journal of Educational Psychology,* 86: 350–59. Quotation from NRP Report on p. 2-40. Quotation for Castle et al. on p. 352.)

McGuinness et al. (1994)

The first-grade teachers in the experimental groups taught the regular curriculum in their respective classes, one in a Montessori school, the other in "a fairly conventional private school." The two experimental groups were used because Diane McGuinness and her colleagues wanted to compare Montessori teaching, which uses a "discovery method," with more "conventional" teaching, in this case a "modified whole language approach" that encouraged "lots of creative writing and the use of invented spelling." In both groups training in various phonemic analysis and manipulation skills was added. The teacher of the control class also used "a modified whole language approach."

In the skills training, given at the beginning of the year, prior to "whole language" teaching, the students received "phonics instruction for both letter-sound and letter-name correspondences." The teacher reviewed phonics, "covering single letters and common digraphs," after which "phonics was not specifically dealt with," in the experimental classes. The control students, however, by following the regular school program, "used phonics worksheets for word families and for isolating individual sounds in words, usually initial consonants."

At the end of first grade, children in all three groups had made substantial gains in performance on tests of word identification and word attack. However, even though the control children advanced at the normal rate on the word identification test, both experimental groups made better gains, gauging by what would have been predicted from the respective initial scores of the groups. Whether this difference had a significant impact on actual reading is unknown because no measures of full-text reading and reading comprehension were used.

Regardless, the Report fails to mention an important finding: at the end of the school year, there were *no* significant differences between the three groups on the phonemic awareness tests. Hence, PA attainment was not related to reading outcome, a finding that runs counter to the Report's fundamental assertion about the benefits of such training. (McGuiness, D., C. McGuiness, and J. Donohue. 1995. "Phonological Training and the Alphabetic Principle: Evidence for Reciprocal Causality." *Reading Research Quarterly*, 30: 830–852. Quotations on pp. 844, 846.)

Chapter 4: Less Than Impressive Effect Sizes

Uhry and Shepherd (1993)

In this study with first graders receiving PA training, "a measure of silent reading comprehension was used in order to see whether treatment emphasizing decoding would have an effect on this far more complex form of reading." Contrary to expectations, "group differences" on the test "were not significant." (Uhry, J., and M. Shepherd. 1993. "Segmentation/Spelling Instruction as Part of a First-Grade Reading Program: Effects on Several Measures of Reading." *Reading Research Quarterly*, 28: 218–233. Quotations on pp. 225, 228.)

Barker and Torgesen (1995)

Following an eight-week study of a skills-training program, first graders in the program attained superior scores over controls on measures of phonological awareness and word recognition. However, the researchers did not overextend the meaning of this very short-term study, emphasizing that "this study was limited in its ability to evaluate the long-term impact" of the "direct phonological awareness training." To overcome this limitation, they encouraged "future studies" to "evaluate" long-term effects.

As in many other studies used in the Report, this one provided no information about the regular instruction the children received, leaving unaddressed the question of the kind of regular instruction the eight weeks of skills training benefited. (Barker, T., and J. Torgesen. 1995. "An Evaluation of Computer-Assisted Instruction in Phonological Awareness with Below Average Readers." *Journal of Educational Computing Research,* 13: 89–103. Quotation on p. 101.)

Hurford et al. (1994)

First graders identified as "at risk for reading disabilities" benefited from a PA training program as measured by tests of PA, word identification, and word attack (using phonics rules). On the latter two tests, however, the score differences between the groups, although statistically significant, were minimal and not what the researchers had anticipated. "Although one could argue that the training significantly impacted the trained students' reading ability," they concluded, "the differences in performance between the trained students and their matched controls were not nearly as impressive as they were on the phonological-processing measures." For example, the researchers expected the untrained reading-disabled controls to score below the standard score level of 90 on the word identification test, but they scored 96.2! (Hurford, D., M. Johnson, P. Nepote, S. Hampton, et al. 1994. "Early Identification and Remediation of Phonological-Processing Deficits in First-Grade Children at Risk for Reading Disabilities." *Journal of Learning Disabilities,* 27: 647–659. Quotation on p. 653.)

Wise et al. (1999)

This study with children with reading difficulties in second to fifth grade used three different phonemic awareness training programs and compared these programs with "regularly scheduled" reading instruction. The students in the training program were taught in groups of three, but the researchers do not say how many students were in the regular classes. We can assume there were many more than three for each teacher.

The researchers did note that "trained students had more personal attention in small groups and more individualization on the computers than would have been possible for most students in the regular-instruction control condition" but did not discuss what impact this difference could have had on achievement outcomes. At the end of the training period, the students in the training groups had scores superior to those of the controls on tests of word identification and word analysis.

We have, then, a study containing a large disparity in teacher-student ratio between the experimental and control groups, a disparity favoring the experimental groups, and no follow-up outcome measures to determine the effects of the training programs on reading achievement for the year following training. (Wise, B., J. Ring, and R. Olson. 1999. "Training Phonological Awareness with and Without Explicit Attention to Articulation." *Journal of Experimental Child Psychology,* 72: 271–304. (Quotation on p. 289.)

Lovett et al. (1994)

This was a study done with "reading-disabled children" to "evaluate the effectiveness of a computer speech-based system for training literacy skills." The training used a "talking" computer program that presented speech sounds in conjunction with written language skills training. Training consisted of twenty-four lessons of individualized instruction in which the children were taught word recognition and spelling of words that were phonetically regular (e.g., *made*) and irregular (e.g., *have*). The program had three versions and on four standardized reading tests, "no reliable treatment effects were revealed." (Lovett, M., R. Barron, J. Forbes, B. Cuksts, and K. Steinbach. 1994. "Computer Speech-Based Training of Literacy Skills in Neurologically Impaired Children: A Controlled Evaluation." *Brain and Language,* 47: 117–154. Quotations on pp. 118, 136.)

Murray (1998)

This three-week study compared kindergartners who received two kinds of phonemic skills training with a control group that engaged in a language experience program in which students composed and later attempted to read stories that they dictated to their teacher, who wrote them on large sheets of paper. Excluded from the language experience instruction was any explicit instruction in "phoneme awareness" and no explicit reference was made to letter identities in the words of the stories the children wrote. Not surprisingly, the groups that were taught phonemic skills did better on tests of phonemic skills than did the control group, for whom all phonemic skills teaching was excluded.

The narrow outcome measures did not include an assessment of story reading, which might have been a strength of the language experience group. (Murray, B. 1998. "Gaining Alphabetic Insight: Is Phoneme Manipulation Skill or Identity Knowledge Causal?" *Journal of Educational Psychology,* 90: 461–475.)

Chapter 5: Systematic Phonics Beats Whole Language!

Responding to my critique of their research, Foorman and her colleagues wrote in *Educational Researcher* that in my reanalysis, I "proceeded to selectively drop classrooms in [their] dataset." After reading this, I sent them the following email (5/31/2000):

> In your paper, "Misrepresentation of Research by Other Researchers," you state, "Coles proceeded to selectively drop classrooms in our dataset." I'd appreciate knowing what classrooms I dropped.

I was first told that I would have to wait for a reply because the coauthor who did most of the statistical analysis was out of town. A few days later, after not hearing from them, I again wrote and this time was told that if I could assure them that their email would not be quoted, they would respond to me. I replied (6/6/2000):

> I'll agree not to quote anything you say beyond simply the identification of the classrooms. In other words, as I understand your statement in the article, there were classrooms I didn't include. Therefore, if you could just give me information for the classrooms and the schools they were in, that will be sufficient. If you think

there's a need to elaborate beyond this, I can assure you I won't quote the elaboration without your permission.

Still not producing any documentation to substantiate their charge, they then answered that they had no interest in communicating with me, to which I responded (6/5/2000):

> Thanks for the clarification. One more question. May I have your permission to [quote], without editing, your entire 6/04/00 email [explaining why you will not give me the information I requested]?

Because that request too was refused, I went on to write (6/5/2000):

> I will simply explain that you would not substantiate your accusation. [As I understand your reply], you won't provide documentation to substantiate your accusation because you [believe] that I won't quote it in its entirety. But when I offer to do so, you won't give me permission [to quote the explanation in full]. I'm sure readers of my next book won't draw the conclusion that you will not substantiate your accusation because you cannot.

As of this writing, Foorman and her colleagues have not published anything that supports their claim about the classrooms I was supposed to have "selectively dropped." (Foorman, B. R., J. M. Fletcher, D. J. Francis, and C. Schatschneider. 2000. "Misrepresentation of Research by Other Researchers." *Educational Researcher,* 29: 27–37. Quotation on p. 31.)

Chapter 6: "These [Phonics] Facts Should Persuade Educators and the Public"

Umbach et al. (1989)

This study with poor, black first graders compared a "traditional basal approach" with a "direct instruction" program, Reading Mastery, that emphasized sound-symbol correspondences, how to blend sounds, and other phonics skills. The children using the basal reading series were instructed in skills but less explicitly and systematically than those in the direct instruction program. At the end of the school year, the direct instruction students scored higher on decoding and reading comprehension tests.

What can we conclude from one more "compared with what?" study? That basal readers are a poor means of learning to read? That direct instruction of skills might be superior to discredited basal readers, at least through first grade? If these were the only alternatives for a school, then direct instruction of skills might be preferred, but beyond this narrow choice, the study tells us nothing about the value of other instructional approaches. (Umbach, B., C. Darch, and G. Halpin. 1989. "Teaching Reading to Low Performing First Graders in Rural Schools: A Comparison of Two Instructional Approaches." *Journal of Instructional Psychology,* 16: 23–30.)

Foorman et al. (1997)

Among groups trained in different forms of phonics programs, and another group taught only sight words, there were some outcome differences in phonics abilities, but no significant group differences on a word reading test, showing that these phonics abilities did not transfer to gains in word reading. (Foorman, B., D. J. Francis, D. Winikates, P. Mehta, C. Schatschneider, and J. Fletcher 1997. "Early Interventions for Children with Reading Disabilities. *Scientific Studies of Reading,* 1: 255–276.)

Greaney et al. (1997)

This study used discredited "whole word" instruction as a control alternative to skills instruction and was designed to show that teaching sound-symbol relationships in beginning reading contributes more to reading development than instruction that purposely avoids teaching them. (Greaney, K., W. Tunmer, and J. Chapman. 1997. "Effects of Rime-Based Orthographic Analogy Training on the Word Recognition Skills of Children with Reading Disability." *Journal of Educational Psychology,* 89: 645–651.)

Leach and Siddall (1990)

This "compared with what?" study examined an evening training session for parents that taught them to use a variety of tutoring methods with their children for ten to fifteen minutes a day. One of the methods was a phonics skills program. Another was "paired reading" (i.e., parents reading with children). Both produced comparable reading test results that were superior to "pause, prompt, praise," and "hearing reading" groups—that is, phonics teaching was not better than reading to children! (Leach, D., and S. Siddall. 1990. "Parental Involvement in the Teaching of Reading: A Comparison of Hearing Reading, Paired Reading, Pause, Prompt, Praise, and Direct Instruction Methods." *British Journal of Educational Psychology,* 60: 349–355.)

Bond et al. (1995–96)

Another "compared with what?" study found that a phonics program produced superior results on word attack skills and letter-word identification tests than were made with a basal reading program. However, the phonics program was not found to be more effective for writing or for oral reading comprehension. (Bond, C., S. Ross, L. Smith, and J. Nunnery. 1995–96. "The Effects of the Sing, Spell, Read, and Write Program on Reading Achievement of Beginning Readers." *Reading Research and Instruction,* 35: 122–141.)

Haskell et al. (1992)

This "compared with what?" study used whole word instruction as a control against skills instruction with first graders. (Haskell, D., B. Foorman, and P. Swank. 1992. "Effects of Three Orthographic/ Phonological Units on First-Grade Reading." *Remedial and Special Education,* 13: 40–49.)

Martinussen and Kirby (1998)

This study compared a phonics-emphasis group with a meaning-emphasis group and with a control group that received no extra instruction. Not surprisingly, the phonics-emphasis group did better on skills tests than did the groups that did not receive skills teaching. Comprehension tests were not used. (Martinussen, R., and J. Kirby. 1998. "Instruction in Successive and Phonological Processing to Improve the Reading Acquisition of At-Risk Kindergarten Children." *Developmental Disabilities Bulletin,* 26: 19–39.)

Vickery et al. (1987)

This study compared remedial classes and "nonremedial classes" over four years. The lack of description of what kind of teaching and learning went on in the nonremedial classes makes test outcomes impossible to interpret. (Vickery, K., V. Reynolds, and S. Cochran. 1987. "Multisensory Teaching Approach for Reading, Spelling, and

Handwriting, Orton-Gillingham Based Curriculum, in a Public School Setting." *Annals of Dyslexia,* 37: 189–200.)

Chapter 7: Encouraging Students to Read More

Burley (1980)

The programmed methods of independent reading practice were (1) programmed textbooks in which students read a selection and then answered questions about the selection read, (2) programmed cassette tapes with which students listened to directions for reading a selection, answered questions, and listened to the tape for the answers, and (3) a method that had students working independently on reading skills.

The Report also notes that there were "no differences on a vocabulary measure," presumably another criticism of the study. However, Burley saw this differently: since the SSR group was more successful than the other three groups and "since neither of the four reading practice methods was significantly different in vocabulary, this lack of difference tends to support rather than adversely affect the overall success of the Sustained Silent Reading Method." In other words, Burley reasoned, all four groups had the same reading vocabulary knowledge, but the SSR group was able to use this knowledge in ways that the other groups did not to improve literal and inferential comprehension. This conclusion is not in the report. (Citation in Endnotes. Quotation for NRP Report on p. 3-25. Quotation for Burley on p. 161.)

Carver and Liebert (1995)

This study set out to test the theory that improvement of a student's reading level comes from reading material at the student's reading level, rather than below it, because at the latter level a student will only maintain his or her reading ability.

Using third through fifth graders in a six-week summer school reading program, researchers Ronald Carver and Robert Liebert tested the hypothesis by having half of the students select library books identified as at or below their reading level, while the other half read books identified as at or slightly above their reading level.

After finding that neither group gained in reading ability, the researchers took a closer look at the reading levels of the books and found errors in their assigned reading levels. The researchers had assumed that the levels designated by the company that sold the collection of books were correct, but their analysis found that, in fact, the books labeled at or below the reading levels of the students were accurately designated, but those books designated to be at or above the students' reading levels were below those levels. Therefore, although most of the students were around grade 5 in reading ability, the ones who were supposed to be reading books at grade levels 5, 6, and 7 in difficulty were in fact reading books around grade levels 3 and 4 in difficulty. As the researchers wrote, "Both groups were reading relatively easy books, and that is the reason there was no support for the reading bootstrap effect." In other words, the researchers were not able to test their hypothesis about the benefits of SSR at one level or another.

As the researchers' themselves explained, the primary variable "supposedly being manipulated in this research, namely, the difficulty level of the books being read, was in fact not manipulated at all." Consequently, "the difference between the so-called easy group and the matched group was more apparent than real. Therefore, with hindsight, it is not surprising that no substantive differences were found" between these two groups. "The failure to find important differences between these two groups in terms of gain in reading ability may be explained by the failure to manipulate the difficulty level of the material being read."

Remarkably, the Report concluded that this research "provided one of the clearest tests of the effect of reading," showing that "these students, in 3rd through 5th grade, made no gains in reading achievement at all, even though the books were at an appropriate level." (Carver, R. P., and R. E. Liebert. 1995. "The Effect of Reading Library Books in Different Levels of Difficulty on Gain in Reading Ability." *Reading Research Quarterly,* 30: 26–48. Quotation for the NRP Report on p. 3-26. Quotations for Carver and Liebert on pp. 43–44.)

Collins (1980)

No differences were found in the students' attitude toward reading, but SSR students appeared to be more overtly responsive to what they read, judging by the higher number of SSR students' verbal expressions of appreciation about what they had read. (Citation in Endnotes.)

Davis (1988)

Unlike most SSR programs, the students in these classes used a single textbook containing short stories, plays, poetry, biographies, and nonfiction. After reading a selection, the students answered questions.

Davis speculated that the results might be related to the text levels and the students' reading levels. For the medium-ability readers, the textbook was closer to their instructional level, that is, the level at which they knew most of the text but had the opportunity to increase their reading abilities by learning a small portion of vocabulary, concepts, facts, genres, and so on. In contrast, the textbook was around the independent level of difficulty for the high-ability readers, that is, the level at which they had mastered the vocabulary, concepts, and so forth and were reading only for reinforcement of what they knew. Consequently, the material was more appropriate for the instructional needs of the medium-ability readers. We will recall that a similar problem in the Carver and Leibert study prevented them from fully testing their hypothesis. Although this study did not set out to do so, it adds support for the Carver and Liebert hypothesis. (Citation in endnotes.)

Evans and Towner (1975)

Fourth graders who read books for twenty minutes daily were compared with others engaged in basal reading instruction that included practicing various reading skills. At the end of the ten weeks, researchers Howard Evans and John Towner found no significant differences on reading tests. A point the Report misses is that the achievement test results did not lend much support to the kind of direct skills instruction that the Report advocates. (Evans, M., and J. C. Towner. 1975. "Sustained Silent Reading: Does It Increase Skills?" *Reading Teacher,* 29: 155–156.)

Langford and Allen (1983)

The study also used three measures of student attitude toward reading, two for students and one for the teachers. On the two student measures, there was no difference between the experimental and control groups in attitude toward reading. On the teachers' instrument, however, which "measured observable behavior patterns reflecting student attitudes toward reading," there was a significant difference. These conflicting outcomes led the researchers to conclude that "it is impossible to draw any conclusions about the relationship of SSR to reading attitudes." Is the glass half empty or half full? This conclusion is not the same as the Report's description that the study found no differences in reading attitude. (Citation in Endnotes.)

Manning and Manning (1984)
In peer interaction, the students "engaged in varied activities such as small group and paired discussions about books, oral reading in pairs, and book sharing through activities such as puppetry and dramatization." The individual conferences with teachers lasted for three to ten minutes per student, and each student conferred with the teacher at least once a week.

If one is looking for research results that could contribute to classroom instruction, one could take from this Manning and Manning study the insight that sustained silent reading that is extended, reinforced, transformed, and amplified in pair reading and discussions deepens comprehension more than fourth-grade students reading alone or just engaged for a longer time in conventional classroom reading instruction. Although the study is limited, its outcomes do not contribute to the Report's general conclusion that it is "unreasonable to conclude that research shows that encouraging reading has a beneficial effect on reading achievement." (Citation in Endnotes. Quotation for the NRP Report on p. 3-29. Quotation for Manning and Manning on pp. 377–378.)

Peak and Dewalt (1994)
The AR students gained an average of 15.3 points on a standardized reading test from grades 3 to 6, compared with a 10.2-point yearly gain for the students who did not use the program. From grades 6 to 8, the AR students gained 13.2 points per year, compared with 5.5 points per year for the control students. (Citation in Endnotes.)

Reutzel and Hollingsworth (1991)
Reutzel and Hollingsworth conclude:

> The fact that trade book reading produced readers who scored as well on the skills test as students receiving instruction and practice on selected comprehension skills raises another important

issue with respect to the continued teaching of reading comprehension skills. In a time when the important contribution of background knowledge to comprehension is well known, it is quite reasonable to expect that wide reading embellished readers' background knowledge and experiences, thus leading to incremental improvements in comprehension.

Following this statement, they cited research that found that spending time in silent reading was associated with reading achievement gains. (Citation in Endnotes. Quotation on p. 42.)

Summers and McClelland (1982)

The researchers studied SSR in classes from fifth through seventh grade during a five-month period and found no significant benefits for SSR in tests of reading achievement and reading attitude. However, they suggested that their data contained some evidence that a "longer treatment period might have been desirable." Some schools took longer to implement the SSR program, thereby achieving "different levels of use" because "start-up activities, in particular, take longer than anticipated, especially when total school efforts are involved."

The researchers also noted, "although the statistical results of the study were nil, interesting educational implications exist," as suggested in the final summary rating questionnaire, which showed that the teachers, librarians, and principals in the SSR schools "reacted favorably to SSR as a curriculum activity" and "rated children's reactions as being very positive overall." Most felt that SSR was "very beneficial in developing reading interests, and almost all rated some increase in the range of topics read as a result of SSR in their classrooms." Most also felt that SSR influenced "development of positive attitude toward reading as a school subject," suggesting "it would benefit the total range of children in intermediate classrooms."

These post-study comments are not meant to dismiss the finding of a lack of significant differences in tests of achievement or attitude. They do, however, suggest that there were some influences, especially in the amount of time needed to implement the program adequately, that could explain why, although there were no statistical benefits, those educators who followed implementation viewed the program as worthwhile. (Summers, E. G., and J. V. McClelland. 1982. "A Field-Based Evaluation of Sustained Silent Reading (SSR) in Intermediate Grades." *Alberta Journal of Educational Research*, 28: 100–112. Quotations on pp. 107, 109.)

Vollands et al. (1999)

The Report criticized the first study for using an "assisted reading" program, which contaminated the AR results.

It is true that a peer-tutoring "assisted reading" program was introduced alongside the AR program after two months of classroom work, but it was used for only two school days each week, beginning with eight pairs of students and declining to only two. Possibly, this did contaminate the research design. However, the researchers stated that they did not believe that the "minimal use" of this intervention had "significantly affected these results." (Citation in Endnotes. Quotation on p. 208.)

Index